KT-482-511

Contents

Notes for teachers and students *vi*

1 · Politics   *1*

What is politics?   *1*
The politics of everyday life   *1*
What is political activity?   *2*
What is power?   *2*
The consensus view   *4*
The conflict view   *5*
Summary   *5*
Questions   *6*

2 · The politics of schooling   *7*

What is the politics of schooling?   *7*
The internal politics of schools   *7*
Local and central government   *10*
Developments in State schooling   *11*
Independent schools   *13*
Summary   *14*
Questions   *14*

3 · The politics of gender   *15*

What is gender?   *15*
Socialization   *16*
Magazines   *18*
Conflict   *19*
Language   *21*
The Sex Discrimination Act   *22*
Gender differences in Parliament   *22*
Patriarchy   *23*
Summary   *23*
Questions   *23*

4 · The politics of the family   *24*

What is the family?   *24*
Politics within the family   *24*
Politics outside the family   *26*
Background to the family in Britain   *28*
Alternatives, the future, and you   *31*
Summary   *32*
Questions   *32*

5 · The politics of racism   *33*

What is race?   *33*
Racism   *33*

The media *34*
Employment *35*
Housing *37*
Education *37*
Background to immigration in Britain *37*
The role of the Government *38*
Ethnic community politics *40*
Summary *40*
Questions *40*

6 · The politics of the mass media *41*

What are the mass media? *41*
Political effects of the mass media *41*
Ownership and control of the media *43*
The mass media and the Government *46*
Alternatives *48*
Summary *50*
Questions *50*

7 · The politics of work *51*

What is work and why do it? *51*
Money and conflict *52*
Why is work important? *53*
Status *54*
The influence of the Government *56*
Trade unions *57*
Alternatives and change *58*
The Lucas Plan: a case study *59*
Summary *60*
Questions *60*

8 · The politics of democracy *61*

What is democracy? *61*
Classical democracy *61*
An ideal or a system? *62*
Elitism *62*
People's democracy *63*
Liberal democracy *64*
Liberal democracy in Britain *66*
Summary *69*
Questions *69*

Extension activities *70*

Glossary *72*

Index *74*

Acknowledgements

The author and publisher would like to thank the following people for permission to reproduce copyright material:

Barnabys pp 2, 26 (btm), 51 (centre btm); BBC Enterprises pp 41, 47; BBC Hulton Picture Library pp 39 (btm), 56 (top); Camera press p 15 (top); Daily Mirror p 34; Format pp 3 (top, Joanne O Brien), 4 (top, Pam Isherwood), 14 (btm), 16 (btm, Jenny Matthews), 19 (top, Pam Isherwood), 20 (top, Brenda Prince), (centre, Maggie Murray), 21 (btm left, Sheila Gray), (btm right, Maggie Murray), 27 (btm, Maggie Murray), 31 (top, Raissa Page), 32 (top, Brenda Prince), 33 (top, Val Wilmer), (btm, Pam Isherwood), 54 (top, Brenda Prince), 58 (top, Brenda Prince), 63 (top, Raissa Page); Keith Gibson pp 39 (top), 51 (btm right); General Mills Toy Group Europe p 17 (btm); Guardian Newspapers Ltd p 47; Richard and Sally Greenhill pp 1 (btm), 9 (top), 13 (top), 15 (btm), 24 (top), 25 (top), 51 (top), 55 (top), 64 (btm); Independent Broadcasting Authority p 44; Mansell pp 7 (btm), 11 (btm), 12 (top), 28, 37, 62; Mary Evans Picture Library p 29 (btm); Mattel

p 17 (btm); National Museum of Labour History p 57 (btm); Network pp 1 (top), 2 (top, Chris Davies), 6 (top, Steve Benbow), 9 (btm, Mike Abrahams), 13 (centre, John Sturrock), 35 (btm), 37 (Mike Abrahams), 51 (btm left, Barry Lewis), 54 (btm, Katlin Arkel), 61 (top, Steve Benbow), 64 (top, John Sturrock), 67 (top, Judah Passow), 68 (top, Mike Abrahams), (btm, Mike Abrahams); The Photo Source pp 29, 30 (btm), 38 (btm), 52, 61; John Powell p 18 (btm left, centre and right); Jill Posener p 16 (top); Plymouth Advertiser p 45; Rex Features pp 15 (btm left), 23 (top), 24 (btm), 27 (top), 50, 66 (top); Time Magazine Inc/ Joe Lertola p 42 (btm); John Topham Picture Library pp 25 (btm), 40 (top), 46, 49 (btm), 63 (centre), 66; Volvo Concessionaires UK p 5 (centre); Yorkshire Post p 48 (top).

Quotations on: p 23, from *Sweet Freedom* by Anna Coote and Beatrix Campbell (Picador 1982); p 28, from *The Family, Sex and Marriage in England, 1500–1800* by Lawrence Stone, (Penguin 1979); p 35, from 'The Mass Media and Racial Conflict' by Paul Hartman and Charles Husband (*Race* Volume 12, No 3, January 1971); p 36, from *Women in the Eighties* (Counter Information Service, Spring 1981); p 38, quoted in *Anglo-Saxons and Celts* by L P Curtis (New York University Press, 1968); p 39 from *Our People* (booklet to supplement Thames Television Programme, January 1979: programme producers Alex Horrox and Gillian McReady).

Illustrations are by Merrily Harpur and Viv Quillin. (Nigel Paige cartoon p 42, top; Helen Cusack drawing p 19, btm right.) Cartoon (p 67) based on figures from an article by Professor Ivor Crewe which appeared in *The Guardian* 13 June 1983.

The cover illustration is by Merrily Harpur.

Notes for teachers and students

People, Power, and Politics introduces areas of political activity with which students are already familiar, but which they might not have considered as being political. The aim of the book is to enable students to recognize the political dimensions of their own lives and to put them into a wider social and political context within contemporary Britain. It is hoped that in recognizing elements of power, control, conflict and decision-making in students' own experience, they will be stimulated to develop their own political attitudes and to take political action where it is possible and appropriate.

The book does not suggest which types of political action are most suitable, nor does it, on the whole, suggest setting up situations in which students can practise political skills. However, teachers and students might want to construct role-play and simulations where a compound of political knowledge, attitudes and skills are developed. Alternatively, they may recognize political issues in their own experiences and in real situations which exist at school, college or in their community, and use these as examples from which to understand political concepts.

Understanding political concepts, developing political attitudes and exercising political skills are all necessary to the process of becoming politically literate. This book in itself does not produce political literacy, but it does try to point to areas where students and teachers can develop a greater awareness of the politics in their own lives and those of others.

A critical approach is needed to this and other sources of political literature and political education. It is not possible to present every point of view or every fact relating to particular situations. A selection has been made and one which is intended to be explicitly anti-racist and anti-sexist. This perspective has informed all the Chapters in the book, but is more apparent in some than in others.

1·Politics

What is politics?

Politics is often thought to be about what governments do. In Britain, people generally assume that politics is about what the Government and the political parties say and do.

> For example, you will probably have heard people say things like:
> 'I never discuss religion, politics or sex.'
> 'Keep politics out of sport.'
> 'Education should have nothing to do with politics.'

In these cases people usually mean 'politics' in a limited sense, as the activities of governments, rulers, professional politicians and political parties. This is an important area of political activity, but it is not the only one.

The politics of everyday life

Everyone has to make decisions; about how to spend money, how to spend their time, whether to please themselves or other people.

> **For example**
> - At school you might be asked to vote at the school council meeting on how to spend the school fund, or you might vote in your form on how to raise money for charity
> - At home you might discuss where to go on holiday or which television programme to watch

These ordinary activities, at home, at school, at work, in clubs or in groups of all kinds, provide an important source of politics; the politics of everyday life.

We are born into some groups. What are they and how can they be political?

We are all members of groups and our society is, at present, divided into groups:
- We are *born* into some groups: our social class (working class, middle class or upper class); our sex (male or female); our ethnic and religious group.
- We *choose* to join other groups: such as clubs, trade unions and friendship groups.

1

What powers do the referee and the captain have?

What is power?

Power is the capacity to get your own way, to control your own life and sometimes the lives of other people too, despite resistance.

Political power is the means by which certain ideals, interests and policies can be put into practice. Within a family this might mean that adults have the power to decide what time children go to bed, and that they can use force to make sure that their power is effective. Parliament has the power to make new laws and it can use the courts to make sure that they are obeyed.

Reward and punishment

Power, in families, schools and governments, includes the ability to reward and to punish. This means that decisions can be taken and put into practice.

Name five groups which you belong to. How are they political?

All of these are areas in which we can take part in politics, through discussion and decision-making. Few of us are involved in politics as Members of **Parliament** (MPs) or as councillors, but all of us are involved in the politics of everyday life.

What is political activity?

Whenever we are members of a group such as a family or a school, where decisions have to be made, resources are allocated and **power** is exercised, we are involved in political activities. In this sense politics includes all of us and many of the things we do. Wherever there are conflicts of interests and values, and these conflicts have to be reconciled so that agreement can be reached, there is political activity.

So, politics is about power and about how decisions are made, and about how disagreements are sorted out. Politics can be about governments, but it is mainly about people.

For example

- Youth club leaders and a committee of members might decide that everyone who comes to the club must pay 20p each time they attend. If someone refuses to pay, the youth club leaders have the power to throw them out or to ban them from the club. Their power consists of both their physical ability and the **authority** given to them by other members of the youth club who do pay.
- School teachers have the power to reward pupils who hand in their homework on time and arrive punctually for lessons by writing good reports for them at the end of term, or giving them good references when they leave school.

Who has decided that these students will wear a school uniform and why?

When Parliament passes an **Act** and this becomes law, the courts have the power to punish people who break it.

Decision-making

So, decision-making is an important way of exercising power. You will have noticed that some individuals and some groups have more power to make decisions than others. Power is not equally distributed in our society.

For example, at school the head teacher has the power to decide that a certain part of the building will be out of bounds to pupils. Teachers will be expected to enforce this decision and pupils who break the rule can be punished. Teachers can make similar decisions, but it would be difficult and unusual for pupils to do so. This is because parents, school governors, other groups in society and pupils themselves have accepted that young people are not as responsible as adults and should not have as much freedom and control over their lives as older people have. This may or may not be true, but it is part of the beliefs and attitudes of our society.

We may not always notice that some people have more power than others. When we do recognize it, we may not understand why and we often take this unequal distribution of power for granted as normal. It is difficult to see how things could be different.

The political aspects of our everyday lives, the arguments and conflicts, the decision-making and the exercise of power, will be seen more clearly when we explore the ways in which different groups of people behave:

- at home
- at school
- at work
- in relation to their gender, their social class and their ethnic (or racial) group

But everyday politics are not separate from the sort of political system in which we live.

The ways we think and behave are influenced by the sort of society in which we live and the way we are governed. There are connections between the ways people behave at home, at school, at work and in government.

For example, the ways in which decisions are made are similar in very different situations:

- In a family, parents and children might talk and argue about what time the children ought to go to bed, but the final decision is usually made by a parent, often the father
- At school, pupils might be consulted about whether or not they should wear school uniform, but the decision is usually taken by the head teacher, who is often a man
- In government, a great deal of discussion takes place before a decision is reached, and here again the decision-makers are mainly men

When these different levels of society are examined, it is clear that similar patterns of power and decision-making exist. The connections between different levels of political activity in society are the beliefs, values and attitudes which are dominant. In these examples we can see that certain ideas about the roles of men and women and the value of discussion in decision-making are dominant in our society, and these operate at all levels of political activity.

What happens when discussions break down?

3

None of these levels of activity are separate in real life because they overlap and interact. What is important is to be able to recognize political disputes and to have some understanding of the main arguments at whatever level they take place.

The ways in which people explain and describe politics will be affected by their view of the world, their beliefs and values and the way they think their society works. Not everybody explains society and politics in the same way. There are two main ways, and although these are not the only ones they are the most common.

The consensus view

People who see society as a reasonably well-functioning machine have a consensus view of society.

On a sewing machine all the parts work together to make the machine run smoothly and efficiently. Similarly, all the main parts of society, institutions like education, the law, the family, industry, the Church and Government, are seen to be working together to make society run smoothly and efficiently.

'Power is authority'

From this view, it is argued that everyone basically agrees about who should have power and how it should be used. Power, in this perspective, is usually seen as authority; that is, power which is accepted by most people as being in the right hands and therefore legitimate. So the power of governments, or parents, or teachers, or men, is seen as legitimate authority because most people accept it, believe in it and assume that these groups are better at being leaders than other people. They are thought to be better equipped to lead and make decisions because they are more

Power or authority?

intelligent, have had the right experiences or training, or are 'born leaders'.

'Inequalities are natural'

From this consensus view inequalities are seen as being natural and the unequal distribution of power as being normal.

> **For example**
> 'Well, it wouldn't do if everyone wanted to run the country.'
> 'They know what they're doing, they're brought up to it.'
> 'The teachers know best.'

These are the sort of comments which people make and which help to justify a few people having a lot of power and most people having very little. From this point of view the lack of power that some groups of people have because of their race, gender or social class is not seen to be as important. It is the personal qualities they are born with or the hard work they put in to achieve a position in society that counts. This is known as **status** – anyone who wants power and status can work hard to achieve it.

This is one way of seeing and understanding society. The other main way is known as the conflict view.

The consensus view and the conflict view getting their come-uppance from the terrible twins, thought and imagination

4

The conflict view

This view of society explains inequalities between groups of people, and the unequal distribution of power, through conflict. From this view, power is seen not as legitimate authority, but as the ability of some groups to dominate society. Occasionally this domination is by force, but more often through the power over people's minds, and especially their values, attitudes and beliefs.

Powerful groups persuade

From this position it is argued that the mass media, such as newspapers, television, cinema etc., and institutions such as schools, are means by which powerful groups can persuade people to accept inequalities as normal, and beliefs which suit the powerful groups can be made popular.

For example

- Many television programmes and most advertisements suggest that it is important to buy more things and to want a bigger or newer washing machine, car, video recorder, hair dryer or cooker. This enables manufacturers to keep producing these goods and to become wealthier
- Schools often teach children that it is important to obey rules, sometimes without questioning whether the rule is a good one

---

This can create an attitude of acceptance and obedience which may make government easier, but might not improve the quality of the lives of the majority of people.

Different groups conflict

The conflicts in society, according to this view, are between different groups:

- middle class and working class
- men and women
- young and old
- black and white
- powerful and powerless

WITH THE VOLVO 340 SPECIAL EDITION WE'VE PANDERED TO YOUR WEAKNESSES.

POWER WINDOWS

ELECTRIC WINDOWS.

5 GEARS.

CENTRAL LOCKING.

PLUSH UPHOLSTERY.

ECONOMY GAUGE.

ECON

AMBIENT TEMPERATURE GAUGE.

CHROME WHEEL TRIMS.

SPECIAL COACHLINE.

CHOICE OF METALLIC FINISHES.

B478 LDX

You may think we've been a bit extravagant with our latest Volvo.

But then again, it is a special edition.

We've included all the extras you've always hankered after, but didn't think you could find on a car of this price.

There's a fifth gear (to save you petrol).

Windows that move at the touch of a switch.

And plush upholstery (so you're really sitting in the lap of luxury).

On the dashboard, there's an economy gauge, to help you drive more fuel efficiently and an ambient temperature gauge (very useful as an early warning of icy conditions on the road).

There's also central locking (to save man-oeuvres inside the car).

Outside, we've finished the car with metallic paint (Silver Grey, Ocean Blue, or Anthracite) and a special coachline.

And there's chrome trim on the wheels.

Though we've taken your weaknesses into account, it isn't fair to assume our car has any.

Like every Volvo, the 340 Special Edition is built around a steel safety cage.

It has crumple zones front and rear, that'll absorb a 30 mph impact.

We've also taken the care to weld a steel bar into the front doors, should you be unfortunate enough to be involved in a side-on collision.

Then to top it off, we've rustproofed the car in a unique 37 stage programme.

The Volvo 340 Special Edition goes for only £5,941.

For which you get the trappings of a luxury car, and a lot of peace of mind.

After all, you may have your soft spots

BUT DON'T THINK WE'VE BECOME SOFT HEARTED.

when it comes to cars, but you also have them when it comes to accidents.

Fortunately, the Volvo 340 Special Edition caters for both.

To: Volvo, Springfield House, Mill Avenue, Bristol BS1 4SA.
Please send me details.

Mr/Mrs/Miss

Address

Postcode

THE 1985 VOLVO 340 SPECIAL EDITION. FROM £5941.

VOLVO 340 SPECIAL EDITION STARTS AT £5,941. PRICES INCLUDE CAR TAX AND VAT (DELIVERY) AND NUMBER PLATES EXTRA) CORRECT AT TIME OF GOING TO PRESS. CUSTOMER INFORMATION TELEPHONE: (IPSWICH (0473) 715151. FOR EXPORT SALES TELEPHONE : 01-493 0355.

What features do Volvo use to sell this car? Why do you think they emphasize safety?

Summary

These two different ways of seeing society, consensus and conflict, are models. They are frameworks or skeletons which help to explain for us why society is as it is and how it could change.

5

What makes old people in our society relatively powerless?

1 Try to remember what people you know have said about politics. What sort of comments do people make about politics? What sort of politics are they usually talking about?

2 You may have heard comments such as these:
   - 'Politics is boring.'
   - 'Politicians are all the same.'
   Why do you think people say things like this?

3 What sort of things can you make decisions about?
   For example:
   - Can you decide what you look like, by controlling how you dress?
   - Can you decide what time you come in?
   - Can you decide who you go out with and where?
   - Can you decide what lessons you do?

4 What sort of people influence your decisions? Do your family, your friends, or people at school with you affect the way you think and behave?

5 What is the difference between power and authority? (Look at the cartoon at the top of page 2.) Who has power over you? Who has authority over you? Do you have power or authority over other people?

6 There is the opportunity for a youth club of which you are a member to go camping for a weekend, and some people want to go to the seaside while others want to go mountain climbing. How can a decision be reached about where to go?

- **The consensus model assumes that society is basically as well organized as it can be. Some people who hold this view would like to see a few changes so that power is more widely distributed, but accept that the present arrangements are as good as they can be.**
- **The conflict model opens up the possibility of change in society through the disputes and disagreements between groups. This model assumes that the unequal distribution of power in many societies is not in the best interests of the majority of people.**
- **Which model people use will affect the way they see society and describe political activities in Britain and in other countries. Sometimes people try to hold both these views or a mixture of them.**

2 · The politics of schooling

What is the politics of schooling?

Many people argue that politics should be kept out of education and that schooling is too important to be part of political debate and decisions. They usually mean by this that <u>party politics</u> should not influence the quality of education which most pupils receive. They feel that whether a local authority is controlled by the Conservative party or the Labour party, or which political party has formed the Government, should not affect the sort of education available.

If we take the definition of politics which was outlined in Chapter One, we can see that politics does affect education, because some people have more power than others in schools and some people are in positions of authority while others are not. It is not difficult to see who has power in a school and who has not!

In this Chapter we are going to consider four main areas:

- the internal politics of schools and learning
- the influences of local and central government on what goes on in schools
- the origins of schooling for the majority of people in Britain
- how politics has affected the development of an education system in Britain

The internal politics of schools

Influences on teaching

What is taught in schools is determined by various factors:

- tradition
- employers
- parents
- teachers
- and to some extent the activities of governments

Tradition

Tradition plays a large part in shaping what is taught in primary and secondary schools in Britain and other countries.

> **For example,** in Britain Religious Education is a compulsory part of schooling. This is because the Church of England has played a major role in providing education, and financed some of the earliest schools.

This tradition of religious elements in schooling has continued. In this case and others, traditions are not haphazard or random; they develop because some people have decided that some things are important. Who decides and what things have been considered important enough to teach in schools are political issues.

CHURCH OF ENGLAND GRAMMAR SCHOOL, ST. KILDA ROAD

A Church of England grammar school in the nineteenth century

The power of the church in Britain has enabled it to continue to influence what is taught even in **state** schools not run by the Church.

Employers

Employers want young people to work for them who have certain skills, such as the ability to read, write and use numbers. Also they want certain types of behaviour like honesty, reliability or the willingness to take orders.

Parents

Parents generally want schools to continue the education they have begun for their children. They want them to learn about the society and the world they live in and be able to contribute towards that society. They expect schools to teach their children facts, give them skills and teach them to behave in acceptable ways.

Teachers

Teachers, particularly in secondary schools, want to introduce young people to certain kinds of knowledge and ways of thinking, such as scientific, mathematic, literary and historical knowledge. They also want their pupils to be able to contribute towards and to fit in to society, as well as to help to change it.

Activities of governments

In Britain, the government department responsible for education, the Department of Education and Science, makes very few rules about what must be taught in schools. Although there are guidelines for the types of knowledge, skills and attitudes which should be made available to pupils at certain ages, local authorities and individual schools have some freedom to decide exactly what is taught and when. The only subject which must be taught is Religious Education.

All of these groups, employers, parents, teachers and the Government, have some power to influence and decide what pupils learn. This power is very important because it also means that they can decide what is *not* taught. Some pupils might think it would be valuable to be able to learn to drive a car, or build a bicycle or mend a television, but few schools offer these kinds of educational experience, and pupils on the whole have little power to influence what they learn.

Influences on learning

Non-teaching staff

The ways in which learning takes place in schools is mainly determined by the teachers, but it is also affected by the non-teaching staff in schools, such as the caretakers and kitchen, office and library staff. The non-teaching staff have the power to affect where and when learning can take place within a school.

For example
- the caretakers may want to have everyone out of the school building by 4.30 p.m. so that it can be locked up for the night. This could mean that activities such as clubs, extra lessons or examination revision cannot take place
- where and when the kitchen staff prepare and serve lunch will affect the use of rooms and the times of the school day
- the librarian may close the library at break times, so that students cannot use the books and other resources outside their lesson times

---

These are important ways in which the learning that takes place in schools is affected by a few people.

Teachers

Teachers probably have the greatest power within a school to influence the ways in which pupils learn.

- In some junior and secondary school classes, children sit in groups at tables and are allowed to talk to each other and help each other with their work. They may decide to follow up a particular area and discuss with the teacher how best they might do this, what resources to use and how to present their findings and the results of their work. They work co-operatively and decide as a group, with the help of the teacher, how to do it. This type of learning is a **democratic** process where the people involved, both teachers and learners, organize their work together, coming to decisions by discussion and sometimes compromise. In this situation the *way* in which learning

The teacher helps the students to organize their own learning

takes place is considered to be as important as *what* is eventually learnt. Teachers can impose sanctions to make sure that learning takes place, such as giving detentions, extra work and by co-operating with parents, but making the work enjoyable and motivating the pupils is seen as the best way to encourage learning.

- Another way of organizing a classroom, which is found in many schools, is for pupils to sit at desks, in straight rows, with the teacher at the front. The teacher talks, and writes on the board, and

pupils only speak to the teacher and not to each other. Often the pupils are only supposed to speak when the teacher allows them to. In this situation, the speed at which the pupils learn, exactly what they learn and how they learn, are all decided by the teacher. The pupils have very little control over their own learning. This type of classroom organization is **autocratic**; that is, one in which the teacher decides for everyone in the class how they will learn without any discussion or consultation about it. The teacher has the power to enforce

this kind of system by using sanctions such as detention, extra work, bad reports to parents or in some cases by using physical force such as the cane.

A further way in which teachers can demonstrate their power in schools is by marking the pupils' work. Teachers decide what is good work and what is bad work, and what is a right answer and what is not. In a few cases pupils are encouraged to assess their own work and that of other pupils. One or a group of pupils may present their work to the rest of the class, who comment on it, making criticism or praising it. Sometimes pupils are taught to assess their own progress by answering questions about how well they have worked, what they have learnt and whether they are improving or not. This form of assessment gives pupils greater control over their own learning and more **autonomy**, that is, self-motivation and the ability to work on their own without constant leadership from teachers, parents or others.

Pupil involvement

Many secondary schools, but few primary schools in Britain, have a school council. This is a formal means by which pupils can take some part in the organization and running of the school. This can give pupils a degree of control over their learning and some power over aspects of school life which affect

The teacher tells the students what he wants them to learn

Where is the teacher?

9

them. However, much depends on the powers given to the school council by the head teacher and teaching staff. In most cases school councils are limited to discussions about the state of the school dinners or the toilets.

Nevertheless the school council can provide an interesting forum for political debate, where **elected representatives** present the views of their tutor group or form group and learn how to chair, minute and influence a committee:

- the person who chairs the meeting must be fair and make sure that everyone has a chance to speak, but no-one speaks too much.
- the person who minutes the meeting must make a brief but accurate account of what was said and decided.
- people at the meeting must learn how to speak clearly in public and in such a way that they convince others of their argument.

Pupils can see how, in school councils, decisions are made by a small group of people on behalf of the majority of people who have elected them. This type of **representative democracy** is typical of many western democratic societies, like Britain, where it is thought to be impossible for everyone to take part in decision-making, so a few people are elected as representatives of the many. Elections are held at regular intervals for voters to elect their Members of Parliament in general elections, and their councillors in local elections.

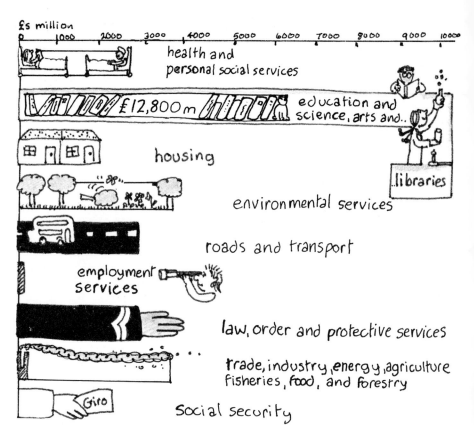

Amounts spent by Local Authorities on Services, 1983–84 (figures for 1986 not available)

Local and central government

- Local authorities are responsible for the general administration of schools in their area. The local authorities provide most of the money for their schools from the rates, a local tax levied on householders and businesses.
- Some money for education, such as the wages for teaching staff, comes from central government funds.

Local authorities

Local education authorities can decide what proportion of the money that they have raised through the rates will be spent on schools and colleges. Usually this is the largest single part of their budget, while housing, planning, public health and family and welfare services receive a far smaller proportion.

The decisions about how much money to spend on schools are made by committees within the local authority. These committees are made up of elected representatives called 'councillors':

- Councillors stand for election every four years.
- Usually they are members of one of the major political parties, but they can also be independents or people concerned with particular local issues and not members of a political party.
- All councillors are responsible to the electorate. The electorate comprises not only the people who voted for the candidate who won the election, but all voters, including those who voted for other candidates. They also have to work with the appropriate central government department, and in the case of education this is the Department of Education and Science (DES).

Central government

Decisions made by central government, like how much money to make available for education, can affect the quality of schooling which a local authority provides. The local authorities depend on central government for some money to help to provide education in their area,

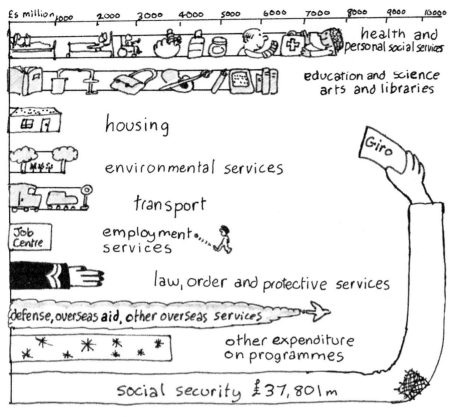

Amounts spent by Central Government on Public Services, 1985–86

even though most of the money comes from local rates. Political parties, such as the Labour party, the Conservative party, the Liberal party or the Social Democratic party (SDP), all have different ideas about how money should be spent. The arguments between the representatives of the political parties, and the way the representatives take sides on the basis of these arguments, are known as party politics.

Party politics affect education in so far as the policies of the major political parties influence the sorts of decisions they make about education and about how much money they spend on it:

- On the whole, the Labour party are prepared to spend a larger proportion of the money raised through taxation on education and welfare services than the Conservative party are. The Labour party support comprehensive secondary education, which does not involve selecting pupils for separate schools according to their ability.
- The Conservative party are less inclined to spend money on

education and more likely to put money into industry, defence and policing. The Conservative party, in general, have shown less support for comprehensive education and are more in favour of the selective system of secondary education, in which pupils go to different schools according to their abilities.

However, all parties agree on the need for some kind of compulsory education system provided for from taxation. This agreement and the provision of State schooling for all is relatively recent.

Developments in State schooling

Origins of schooling in Britain

Until the beginning of the twentieth century, there were very few opportunities for most people to go to school.

- Some schools were available to the sons of the very wealthy who

could afford to pay fees at private schools. There were almost no places for girls at such schools. It was not considered necessary, and indeed it was often thought of as positively harmful, to educate girls at school.
- Church schools existed, which also charged fees, but they tended to be less expensive than the private and grammar schools.
- There were also some small private schools and charity schools: such as the dame schools, run by unmarried, middle class women; and the ragged schools, so called because the children wore torn and ragged clothes because they were very poor. These schools were available for the less wealthy, but even they made a charge to pupils and only managed to survive by having large classes, poor conditions and low standards.
- Some factory schools, which were set up and run by employers, existed.
- Sunday schools provided a minimum education for children who worked all week. They were run by local churches and provided schooling on a Sunday.
- None of these aimed to provide working class children with more than the ability to read the Bible, to obey simple instructions and to develop 'habits of industry and

A dame school

11

A ragged school

The Butler Education Act provided for free secondary education for all. According to the 1944 Education Act, all children would leave their primary schools at 11 years old after taking an examination. The examination, known as the '11 plus', was used to decide which pupils went to which type of school:

- the academic pupils would go to the *grammar schools*.
- The pupils interested in craft subjects would go to the new *technical schools*.
- The rest would go to the *secondary modern schools*.

It was intended that each of these types of schools would be equal in status, but offer different types of education for different types of pupils. The school leaving age was raised to fifteen and later to sixteen years.

piety'. Many children received no schooling at all.

Government involvement

In 1870, the Government began to take a more active part in the provision of schooling:

- They set up elementary (or primary) schools in areas where there were no other schools.
- Church schools were given government money to help them to provide more places.
- In 1918, the school leaving age was raised from 11 to 14 years old.
- More secondary schools were built to cater for the large numbers of children whose parents could not afford to send their children to grammar schools, which still charged fees.

Reasons for change

These were the beginnings of free, compulsory education in Britain. What were the reasons for these changes taking place?

- On the one hand, it is claimed that working class pressure and middle class activists fought for and won the right for all children to receive schooling regardless of income and ability to pay, in much the same way as it is said working

class men and later women won the right to vote.

- On the other hand, it is claimed that working class people were given the right to be educated so that their ignorance would not be a danger or a threat to their masters, the factory owners and the Government. If they could read the Bible and understand enough to be able to vote, they might not become an unruly and dangerous mob.

It is likely that changes in the provision of schooling came about as a result of both of these kinds of pressures.

The tripartite system

The most significant recent development in state schooling took place in 1944. The coalition Government (1940–45), which included Conservative, Labour and Liberal MPs working together through the war years, passed the Butler Education Act.

There were doubts about the 11 plus examination and about sending pupils to different schools according to their 'age, ability and aptitude' from the start. Some local authorities preferred to develop comprehensive secondary schools as an extension of the primary schools, where pupils of all abilities were catered for. It was soon clear that the three types of schools were not equal. The grammar schools were the ones with status and prestige where children mostly from middle class families went; the secondary modern schools were predominantly for children from working class homes and few went on to higher education or top jobs.

One reason suggested for this division by social class and not by ability is that schools are middle class institutions and so favour children from middle class backgrounds. Teachers are predominantly middle class, white and, in secondary schools, male. People have different views on this.

- On the one hand it is claimed that from their positions of power within schools teacher's values, beliefs and attitudes make up the character of the school in general.
- On the other hand it is said that schools are neutral institutions and only pass on knowledge and generally accepted standards of behaviour.

It is likely that this knowledge taught and the attitudes encouraged are a selection from many. This selection often ignores the history and experiences of working class pupils and pupils from ethnic minority groups. There is evidence from examination results that working class pupils and pupils from some ethnic minority groups are not doing as well as they ought, even in the comprehensive system of education.

By the 1960s, there was mounting evidence that the **tripartite system** of grammar, technical and secondary modern schools was not working, and in particular, that working class children were failing in this system. What was against this system? The Labour Government argued that:

- There was a wastage of ability because too many working class children were failing the 11 plus examination and going to secondary modern schools. There they did not receive the same status and educational success as pupils in the grammar schools who were aiming for public examinations and higher education.
- To divide people according to their social class, or even according to their ability (as it was measured by the 11 plus examination) gave the children in the secondary modern schools an unequal and less favourable chance in life. Working class children in secondary modern schools had very few opportunities to go on to higher education and managerial or professional jobs later.
- This was a loss to the country as a whole as well as a disadvantage to the children themselves.

Comprehensive schools

The Government issued a circular to all local authorities encouraging them to reorganize their secondary schools along comprehensive lines in the interests of social equality and industrial efficiency.

- Local authorities controlled by Labour councillors were prepared to make these changes and several, such as Croydon and Leicestershire, had already done so.
- Conservative controlled councils were slower to make changes. Some firmly refused to present

Students at a comprehensive secondary school in the 1980s. Can you predict what kinds of jobs they might go into?

Students at Eton, a famous and exclusive public school, in the 1980s. What sorts of jobs would you expect them to go into?

plans for moving towards comprehensive schooling or delayed drawing up plans, probably in the hope that the Government would change and a Conservative Government would retain selection at 11.

- Nevertheless, by the late 1970s most local education authorities had reorganized their secondary schools so that most students in State secondary schools in Britain are in comprehensive schools.

Independent schools

State schools are not the only form of schooling in Britain. Independent schools also exist, where the parents of pupils pay fees to the school for their children's education. There are alternative (such as Steiner schools) and religious (such as Jewish and Muslim) independent schools.

Public schools are among the oldest fee-paying schools in Britain. Many existed long before schools were provided by the State and financed

13

from taxes. The fees which parents pay vary according to the school and whether or not the pupil is a boarder and stays there all term or a day pupil and lives at home. Few people can afford the fees.

Only a small proportion of the total school population is in public schools, and only about 2½ per cent of all fourteen year olds attend public school. However, a disproportionate number of the most important and powerful jobs in our society are held by people who have attended public schools. Why is this?

- Some people argue that this is because they have received a better education and one which equips them to become leaders.
- Others argue that the name of the school alone impresses employers and so provides their pupils with more opportunities.

Summary

Schooling is political. Within schools there are differences in distribution of and access to power. Teachers, pupils and parents do not all have the same degree of control over learning and there are political arguments in most schools about how learning should take place.

Local and central government have some political control over schools through the amount of money they make available for education and their policies on how it should be used.

The history of State schooling shows that over the last hundred years political decisions have been made which have deeply affected the type of school system we have in Britain today. The workings of this system can be influenced by people who are not necessarily in positions of central authority. In schools, teachers are accountable to parents, governors, the local authority and the DES. Governments and local authority councillors are elected by the voters, and they are answerable to the electorate. By voting and in situations where we can be directly involved, such as at school and in the school council, we can take part in politics, discuss issues, make decisions and hold or share power.

1 Who has power over you at school? What sort of people influence your day at school and how? Think about teachers, prefects, caretakers, kitchen staff, etc.

2 What do you think is the difference between *power* and *authority*? Can you give examples of each from this Chapter?

3 Find out what staff committees there are in your school. What are they trying to do? Are students involved in these committees?

4 In a group write a **constitution** for a school council. This should answer the following questions:
- Who can come to the school council meetings? Should it be everyone, or some pupils, teachers and non-teaching staff?
- If not everyone, how will people be chosen? Will they be elected, or self-appointed?
- How often will the council meet?
- Who will call the meetings, and how will they be run?
- Will someone chair and minute meetings? Who?
- What powers will the school council have?
- What can it discuss? Should it consider school dinners, lessons, money?
- What can the school council do to enforce its decisions?

5 Choose one person in the group to be the school keeper, janitor or caretaker, and another to be the judo teacher. The rest of the group will be the members of a judo class who usually use the school gym from 4 p.m. until 5 p.m. on Tuesday. This Tuesday, the caretaker wants to close the gym at 3.45 p.m. so new lines can be painted on the floor. In role-play, argue your case to reach a solution.

State schooling depends on public money which is controlled by governments. What happens if governments want to spend less money on education?

3 · The politics of gender

What is gender?

Gender is a term used to describe the difference between men and women which result from and are influenced by the culture and society they live in. What distinguishes between *gender* differences and *sexual* differences is that the latter are biological and physiological differences between women and men. The politics of sex would be about these biological differences and about sexual activity between people. This Chapter is concerned with the gender differences and the politics associated with the ways in which women and men grow up and lead different sorts of lives.

There are a number of popular images of men and women: 'the dumb blonde', the 'ugly mother-in-law', the 'smart young business

The media image of rambo is hard, violent and dangerous. He isn't shown in films as caring or sensitive. Can you imagine him changing a nappy?

executive', the 'tough guy'. These images are **stereotypes**. They do not necessarily exist in real life, but they are pictures of whole groups of people which are built up, often by television and advertisements, and are given a reality which many people take as the truth. If we accept these stereotyped images and act upon the assumptions they make (for example, that all women make bad drivers, or that all men are strong and unemotional – 'big boys don't cry'), we may be in danger of ignoring important aspects of people's personalities. We may ignore the differences and similarities between people because we already have a picture in our minds about what 'that sort of person' – women drivers, teenagers, business men – are like and how they will behave.

The media image of Marilyn Monroe was beautiful and brainless. She wasn't shown in films as intelligent and capable. Can you imagine her changing a plug?

Dame Edna confuses the images of men and women, but, like the 'pantomime dame' and the 'ugly-mother-in-law, creates a stereotype

15

How does the original advertisement exploit women? What does the graffiti tell you about the reaction of some women to adverts like this?

Socialization is the process of learning how to fit in and be acceptable to a particular group in society. Socialization begins at birth and continues as long as we are involved with other people. The politics of gender begins at birth.

Children and the politics of gender

The first question when a baby is born is, 'Is it a girl or a boy?' Why is this important at such an early age? Sex, the reproductive function of boys and girls, is not thought to be important in babies, but gender, the social difference between girls and boys, is. People treat baby girls differently from baby boys:

For example, 'A small extension of [an earlier] experiment was conducted at Sussex University to test the responses of mothers to other people's babies. Again, the . . . baby was presented to a series of women as "he" or "she" and the resultant relationships filmed. It is not particularly startling to know that these women chose sex-stereotype toys to amuse what they took to be boy or girl babies. A manly hammer for "him", a soft dolly for "her"; but what was quite staggering was the way they interpreted identical behaviour by the baby when they thought "he" was a boy, and when they took "her" to be a girl. When "he" became restless and started to wriggle, they assumed he was feeling energetic and wanted to play and so went along with his wishes. When "she" made the same movements, they were interpreted as distress signals and the baby was soothed down.'

From an article by Sally Vincent, *Sunday Times,* 19 February 1984.

For example, when women are portrayed in magazines, advertisements and films as soft, emotional, delicate and scatterbrained, they may begin to see themselves and other women like that, without recognizing other aspects of their lives and personalities. These other aspects may not be allowed to develop because they are not considered to be 'feminine' or suitable for a woman. In the same way, men are often shown as strong, active and unemotional. This stereotyped idea of masculinity means that men who do cry, who are dainty, gentle or caring, are not considered to be 'real men'.

- We will also look at the wider meaning of gender; the social and political differences in society between men and women, especially the differences in power, status and influence of women and men. Government legislation, the Equal Pay Act and the Sex Discrimination Act will be considered as part of the moves towards changing the balance of power between the sexes on the basis of gender.

The creation of such stereotypes can limit our potential if we accept these images, and they can restrict our view of others. The politics of gender is concerned with how these stereotypes of women and men affect our lives, how such images are created and how they can be challenged or changed.

- We need to consider the ways in which girls and boys are brought up: the influences of toys, parents' attitudes, the language we use, magazines and television. The personal area of family and friends is an important one, in which the unequal distribution of power and resources between girls and boys can be illustrated clearly.

What is a 'real man'?

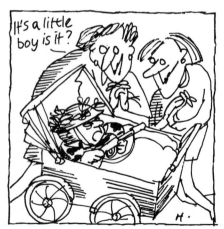

As the baby grows up, parents, relatives and friends begin to give the child certain characteristics: 'Isn't he a big strong boy?', or 'What a pretty little girl!'. As the baby grows into a toddler, these differences continue to be stressed.

The toys and children's books available emphasize these gender differences, and teach children through play what roles they are likely to be expected to fulfil when they grow up.

- Dolls for girls are often baby dolls, which cry and wet their nappies, so that girls learn how to handle, dress and change babies.

- Dolls for boys are rarely even called 'dolls', but are toy 'men' with guns, combat jackets, hand grenades and other weapons.

- Toys such as nurses' uniforms, dolls' houses, sewing sets, toy ironing boards and vacuum cleaners are sold and advertised for girls in particular.

- Garages, building sets, train sets and cars are clearly aimed at boys in the way they are packaged, advertised and promoted.

- Children's books often present boys doing exciting, adventurous and dangerous things while girls are more often shown to be at home and applauding the boys for their bravery.

Both the advertisements and the toys themselves have considerable influence over the things young children learn and how they behave when they grow up. Girls learn how to hold and care for babies and to take trouble over their appearance, by playing with make-up and dressing up. Boys learn how to be aggressive, how to make decisions and deal with machinery.

It is not surprising that being brought up in these ways often produces women who are expected and expect themselves to stay at home, and men who are expected to be brave, enterprising leaders.

What are gender differences?

It is not new to point out the different ways in which boys and girls are brought up, but it is worth doing so to remind ourselves that gender differences do exist.

It is worth noticing that
- Gender differences are not determined by sex differences. Boys are not physically unable to iron, clean, hold babies and change nappies, any more than girls are unable to mend engines or climb trees. Differences in sex are about the reproductive functions of men and women.
- Gender differences are about how women and men are brought up differently, treated differently and expected to behave differently. Gender differences are part of the social, economic and political life of a society.

In most political and economic relations between women and men, it is men who have more power than women. We have seen that in early childhood boys and girls are treated differently.

- These differences and the stereotypes of masculinity and femininity which exist in our society are part of a wider political process which creates inequalities, not just differences.

- Men and women are not 'equal but different'. They are brought up differently and as a result may have unequal life chances, choices and access to power.

- The unequal life chances women and men might have are closely linked to ideas and stereotypes of masculinity and femininity.

- These stereotypes encourage the idea that men are better suited to more important roles outside the home like leading countries, having well-paid jobs or making decisions.

What are the differences between 'girls' dolls' and 'boys' dolls'?

- Women may have power inside the home, but these stereotypes can help to deny that the home and child rearing are important.

It is this political dimension to gender differences that we shall look at.

Magazines

Girls and boys

Teenage magazines provide an example of how girls and boys are seen, and see themselves, differently. Popular magazines for girls and young women between the ages of twelve and twenty all have a very similar layout and format:

- love stories
- problem pages
- features on fashion, beauty and famous people, horoscopes

In the love stories, young women are generally presented as being obsessed with finding and keeping a man. They are often in competition with other girls for a particular man and the stories usually end happily with a man or sadly alone. Rarely are girls shown in strong supportive relations with other girls and hardly ever as having interests in other areas of their lives like work, sport, examinations, or creative activities, unless it is likely to lead them to romance.

Occupations of women and men in Britain, 1984

Magazines for smaller children show girls being successful in a wide range of activities such as horse riding, skating and at school. Girls are shown doing brave and exciting things on their own or with other girls. It is the teenage magazines which show a limited view of girls, and one which does not necessarily reflect their real lives or real interests in school life, sport and getting a job.

In the problem pages of the teenage magazines, the advice given is often intended to lead the girls to be more attractive to men, and horoscopes are generally about possible relations with men. The assumption is that women's lives revolve around men and their main wish is to please men. By contrast, magazines for boys never concentrate exclusively on pleasing girls, finding girl friends and on making boys attractive to girls. Most magazines intended for boys and young men are either about specific activities such as fishing, car mechanics, football or other hobbies and sports, or they contain adventure stories about war and space travel. They do not have problem pages or features on fashion and beauty.

Is this the only way in which girls find happiness and enjoy themselves in real life?

Magazines rarely show girls being creative and happy together

not presented by the media as the same for men and women.

Of course, not all young men want to become soldiers or explorers, and many who want to are not able to. Young women do have thoughts and ambitions other than romantic ones. People do not just conform to images of themselves presented in magazines. It is because these images are often stereotypes and not real pictures of people's lives that conflicts arise.

Conflict

In the home

In the home there may be conflict between brothers and sisters, husbands and wives, or parents and children, about who should do what. It is in the home that the *personal* politics of gender operate. Conflicts about who should wash up, make the beds or hoover are not easy to resolve. Households vary in the ways such jobs are allocated and the ways in which decisions are made:

- In some cases reason is applied so that the housework is shared according to who has the most time and energy to do it. This may mean that the women do not automatically do it if their other jobs mean that they are out of the home a lot or too tired to do it when they come home.

Choice and control

This particular area of the mass media illustrates the way in which girls are presented with a very narrow definition of themselves, almost always in relation to men, while boys are presented with a variety of images; soldier, footballer, space traveller etc. Boys are shown exercising a much greater degree of control over their own lives and over the lives of others than girls are able

to do. The sphere of activity and control for girls is restricted to their emotional lives and their relations with men.

We can see that young men are presented with choices and the possibility of controlling their own lives, while young women are presented with the possiblity of having their lives controlled by men, or of being sad and lonely. These concepts of choice and control are important political ideals, which are

Magazines for boys show them having the freedom to do exciting things outside the house

According to this cartoon, where is the woman's place?

- In other cases parents use their authority to insist that children clean their own rooms and share in general tasks. The children may do it because they simply accept the authority of their parents without question, or because sanctions are applied if they do not, or because they respect the authority of their parents and the reasons behind the decisions. Children may agree to come in at a certain time either because they know they will not be allowed to go out again for some time, or because they know their parents will worry, if they stay out later than this.

Parents can **manipulate** others in the household in order to produce obedience. Manipulation means that the information which other members of the household receive is restricted or distorted.

> **For example,** the father can tell them about the past, 'My mother always did the cleaning and she didn't complain. She was grateful and pleased to clean for my father'; or he can restrict the amount of money available to the rest of the family if he controls pocket money or housekeeping money.

In some cases families resolve conflicts through the use of force and violence.

Sexual violence

> In 1980 male violence was highlighted when the case of the Yorkshire Ripper, a man who raped and murdered thirteen women in the Leeds area, made the news. Women in the area were warned not to go out without the protection of a man, and yet many argued that it was protection *from* men, not by men, that they sought.

In November 1980, a conference on sexual violence was held in Leeds, which brought together a number of different women's groups. They formed a new campaign called 'Women against Violence against Women'. This began a new stage in the debate about the politics of gender: male violence, including rape, assault and battering, were identified as part of the same political structure of dominance and control by men over the lives of women.

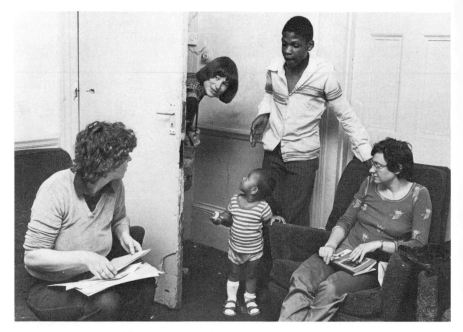

Violence in the home is difficult to escape. Women's refuges make it possible for some women and their children

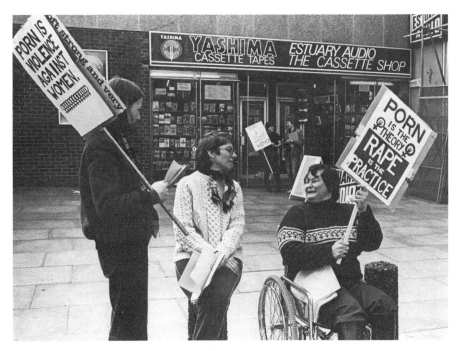

What are the connections between violence against women and pornography?

> 'We agreed that as women gain greater independence, so men use more sexual violence to maintain their position of power over women. Sexual harassment at work undermines our confidence; rape and sexual assault keep us off the streets; sexual abuse in the family cripples our lives and teaches us our place in the world.'
>
> From a report of the conference in *Spare Rib* 103, February 1981.

Reasons

There is disagreement about the reasons for and the extent of male violence.

- Some people argue that all men are potential rapists and violence is part of all men.
- Others assert that men's violence is a symptom of the political relationships between men and

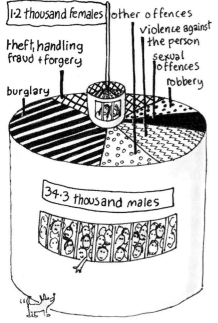

Types of prison sentences for women and men in Britain in 1984

women, so that violence is one way in which men can maintain their superior position, and the way which is used when that superiority and dominance is threatened. As long as women comply with or consent to men's wishes there is no need for violence. Male violence emerges more strongly when women dissent and refuse to accept male superiority.

- Another argument is that male violence is the result of the way in which boys are brought up. Aggressiveness and violence are encouraged and if child rearing practices changed, then men would not behave so violently when they grow up.
- It is also argued that male violence, especially rape, is a psychological and not a political issue, that men who commit such acts are sick and in need of treatment.

These last two positions ignore the social and political contexts in which violence against women occurs, so that broader issues about the unequal distribution of power, status, wealth and incomes between men and women are left unquestioned. Nevertheless, all explanations of conflict and violence agree that men are usually the aggressors and women the victims.

Unfortunately when men do try to be more caring and less aggressive they are often ridiculed by other men. Looking after children, doing housework, and showing emotions are not part of the stereotype of masculinity. Why do you think such men are laughed at or called names?

Language

A major social area in which the politics of gender can be illustrated is that of language.

What is it?

Language is a social construction: we make it, change it and develop it as we use it. People reproduce language they have heard or read, and change it to contain new meanings, so that it is dynamic or open to movement and not fixed or given. When the uses and forms of language change they do so not randomly or by chance, but through the power of particular groups that influence our thoughts and expressions.

For example, new words are introduced to describe new technological developments, like 'space ships', 'microelectronics', 'astronauts' or 'video cassette'. Words which describe new concepts or ideas are also introduced, and it may be that old words are given new meanings. The phrases 'low achievers' or 'low ability' to describe pupils who do not do well at school are terms which have come into use since the growth of mass schooling. It is important to note that it is not the pupils themselves who have introduced these terms to describe their own lack of school success, but people like teachers, educationalists and sociologists, who are in a powerful position to impose new meanings.

This shows how powerful groups can change language and meanings. These groups with power to create new concepts and meanings are usually in positions where their opinions are accepted and where they have access to the media, television, newspapers or publishing, so their views have a wide audience.

Who controls it?

It is argued that men are a powerful group whose power and control is reflected in much of our language. Words and phrases such as 'man-made', 'chairman' and 'a man and his wife' either ignore women and assume everyone is a man, or they suggest that women are entirely dependent on men.

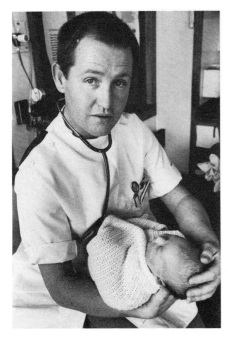

Are there any reasons why he can't do this job? Why don't more boys do this?

Are there any reasons why she can't do this job? Why don't more girls do this?

21

For example, Dale Spender in her book, *Man-made Language*, shows the many ways in which men have created our language and their influence over the lives as well as the language of women. Many women are trying to change **sexism** in language so that women are no longer invisible. One way is to use 'she/he' instead of just 'he' when the sex of a child or adult is unknown. In Marge Piercey's novel, *Woman on the Edge of Time*, there is an imaginary society in which women and men are equal in all respects. There are no pronouns like 'he' or 'she', and instead everyone is called 'per'; For example, 'Per has gone to the shops'. This could refer to a man or a woman, but it does not matter to know which and so no difference is made in the language. Another way is to change the prefixes 'Miss' or 'Mrs' to 'Ms', so that women have one title whatever their marital status, just as men do.

Changes in the weekly earnings of women and men between 1970 and 1984

The process of changing language is linked with changes in the social and political position of women. A lot more discussion about sexism in language has taken place as a result of the women's movement in the 1960s and 1970s, while other changes have been taking place in the relationships between women and men at home, at work and in other social contexts.

The Sex Discrimination Act

In order to help even up the balance of power between men and women in some major areas of social life, and because of pressure from women, the Sex Discrimination Act was passed in 1975. This was an important step made by women in the political progress towards equality.

The political struggle to introduce a law making it illegal to discriminate between people on the grounds of sex had begun in 1967 when Joyce Butler, a Labour MP, introduced a **private member's bill**. It did not become law, but similar bills were introduced almost every year until 1975, when the Labour Government's Sex Discrimination

Bill was passed and became an Act of Parliament. This law makes it illegal to discriminate against people because of their sex or marital status in:

- education
- employment and training
- housing
- the provision of goods and services

The Equal Opportunities Commission (**EOC**) was set up to enforce the Sex Discrimination Act and the Equal Pay Act, which had been passed in 1970 and made it illegal to pay different rates to women and men for doing work which is the same or broadly similar. The EOC was also set up to:

- conduct formal investigations where sex discrimination is suspected
- combat discrimination and promote equal opportunities
- conduct research into relevant areas
- make recommendations to the Government for further changes in areas not yet covered by the law, such as taxation, pension rights, social security and immigration

The EOC is supported by an annual budget of £2 million and a staff of almost 2000 people. Many of the hopes for the EOC have not been realized. The machinery for lodging a complaint of discrimination is complicated, time-consuming and expensive. Of the few cases brought each year only a small proportion are successful.

One of the reasons suggested for the lack of success of the EOC, and for the continued powerlessness of women compared with men, is that the Sex Discrimination Act was drafted largely by men and passed in a Parliament dominated by men. More women in Parliament might influence the kind of legislation passed and the sort of issues debated. It would certainly mean more power in the hands of women.

Gender differences in Parliament

Nineteen women were returned to Parliament in 1979, the year in which Mrs Thatcher became Prime Minister. This was the smallest proportion of women MPs for twenty years. In 1970 there were 26 women MPs out of a total of 635 MPs.

There are a number of reasons why so few women have become MPs:

- Women have a very recent history of recognized party political activity, having only won the right for all women to vote in 1928.
- They are not encouraged as children to seek power, to speak

What would this picture be like if Nancy Reagan was President of the USA instead of Ronald Reagan?

out in public or to express strongly held opinions.

- The way in which Parliament conducts its business, starting in the afternoon and often going on late into the night, is least suited to women when they are often responsible for looking after children.

The few women who have become MPs have not managed to make it easier for more women to do so:

- They have been spread between the major political parties and so their differences of policy have often prevented them from uniting in a campaign to increase the numbers of women in Parliament.
- In some cases women who have reached positions of political power argue that if they can do it anyone can, and the only obstacles are the women themselves, who do not try hard enough to achieve political power.

Patriarchy

The severe shortage of women in the most obvious political arena in British society, Parliament, is an indication of the extent to which our society is based on **patriarchy**.

Patriarchy means a society ruled by the fathers, and has come to mean a society in which men have power over women. Many feminist writers have given explanations of the powers men have and the more limited powers of women, both historically and in modern British society. They have tried to highlight the **exploitation** of women in a culture which is to a large extent dominated by men, and by values and attitudes which maintain the power of men.

Summary

Despite changes in the law, such as the Sex Discrimination Act and the existence of the EOC, women are still in a relatively powerless position in Britain. There are exceptions to this, such as Margaret Thatcher, the leader of the Conservative Party and Prime Minister. The power and status which she has are not typical of women or men. However, the position of women in general, their power and influence has changed and most noticeably in their everyday lives and concerns – in the politics of everyday life.

Many women have been influenced by the women's movement, especially through action over specific and often local issues (such as child-care provision or refuges for battered women) and have become actively involved in politics. Many had not been involved in politics at a party political level. But through the extension of personal politics they have begun to see themselves and the issues about which they care in a wider political context. The way in which women have been able to do this has been by working together, often in loosely-knit small groups, talking together, sharing experiences and supporting each other. This

activity is called 'consciousness-raising'.

'What is important is that we continue to learn and to change ourselves, and that we support each other in this. Consciousness-raising ... stresses the need for every participant to work out her politics for herself, in a supportive context, rather than to receive wisdom from above. It fosters solidarity. It makes personal experiences the base on which theory and strategy are built ... Consciousness-raising is action. ... We are struggling within the family, with parents, children, siblings, husbands – to transform oppressive relationships, to change patterns of behaviour, to redistribute labour and wealth.'

From *Sweet Freedom* by Anna Coote and Beatrix Campbell.

Changes in the law, such as the Sex Discrimination Act, have made this struggle for change and equality more acceptable, but it is the actions of men and women at home, at work and in their everyday lives, as well as the actions of Government, which create political changes.

1 What is the difference between *sex* and *gender*?

2 You are choosing Christmas presents for two small children, a girl and a boy. What would you choose for each? Would you buy the girl a football? Would you buy the boy a doll that cries and wets its nappies? If you did, what might the children each learn from their presents?

3 Why do you think some parents refuse to buy their children toy guns, grenades and other weapons?

4 Write a story for children in which a girl character is gentle and kind and also does brave, exciting and adventurous things.

5 From one copy of a national daily paper count the number of articles which describe male violence such as attacks, fights, shooting etc., and count those articles describing violence by women.

- Do you think the number of crimes and types of crimes reported in the papers is a true reflection of violence in society?
- Do you think women behave as violently as men in general? Why?

6 Make a list of daily and weekly household tasks to be done in a family where there is one adult who works full-time, two teenagers, of whom one is unemployed and the other is at school, and a small child in primary school. Allocate each person daily and weekly jobs and explain why you have given particular tasks to each person.

4 · The politics of the family

What is the family?

The popular image of the family in the West is of a man and a woman, married with two or three children. Television advertisements, magazines, romantic novels and films often promote this picture of the happy <u>nuclear family</u>. Usually the husband goes out to work and supports his wife and their children financially.

This popular image is not the same as many people's experiences of family life. In fact, less than 15 per cent of households in Britain are composed of a man with dependent wife and children living together. There are other ways of living together and bringing up children which are common in Britain and other societies:

Why do many women have two jobs, one paid and one unpaid?

- In many households both parents go out to work to support the family financially.
- In a significant number of households neither parent has paid employment.

- A large number of households have one parent and not two.
- In some cases grandparents live with their children and grandchildren, forming an <u>extended family</u>.
- Some people live in communes where several adults share the responsibility of bringing up the children and running the home.

We shall consider these types of family life, or ways of living together and rearing children, in this Chapter.

Politics within the family

Who has power in a family will depend on how the family is organized. This will be determined to

How typical is this happy nuclear family?

Typical households between 1961 and 1982

some extent on the way the society of which it is a part is organized.

The patriarchal nuclear family

The nuclear family in a patriarchal society, such as Britain and most western industrial societies, is one where the father usually has most power in a family. He often controls the resources of the family, especially when he is the main or only breadwinner. This power over the family's money enables him to:

- make decisions like where to live, where to go for holidays and what to do in leisure time. Even when the father is no longer working and earning money, either through unemployment or retirement, he often retains his power and his control over resources.

- influence the lives of other people in his immediate or nuclear family. He may use this power to decide how his wife and children behave, where they go, who with and when. His decisions can be enforced by applying sanctions, such as withholding pocket money or housekeeping money, or in extreme cases by force and the use of violence.

The symmetrical family

In other families, where there are two parents and both share in decision-making, power resides with the man and woman equally. In some cases the children are also included in

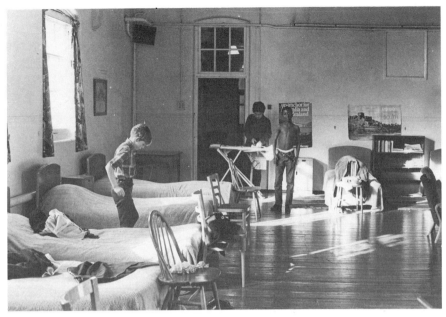

This is a community home where a number of adults and children live together. Is it important for people to have space of their own?

discussions about what to do and how or when to do it. Willmott and Young (two sociologists) describe this as the 'symmetrical family'. It does not mean that everything is shared in the family, but that power is divided more equally. This is usually between the adults, although in some cases this may mean that all adults and children discuss how money should be spent, how time should be used and work should be distributed between members of the household. It may be that each person has an equal say in the decision-making process.

For example, AS Neill tried to run his school, Summerhill, in a directly democratic way such as this when he established it in the 1920s. He regarded his pupils as members of a large family, where everyone took an equal part in making rules and in enforcing them. For instance, everyone would meet to decide whether or not children under ten years old should be allowed to smoke. If a rule was made and then someone broke it, the whole school would meet to decide how the offender should be punished, if at all.

This kind of **participative direct democracy** is not common in schools or families. More often a form of **consultative democracy** exists, in which children are asked their opinions, but eventually decisions are made by the adults. This is because the adults probably have more control over the family's resources, its income, money and property, and they have greater responsibilities for ensuring that all members of the family are safe and healthy. Their greater experience and knowledge are also part of the resources which enable them to do this.

One-parent families

In families where there is one adult, often the mother, but sometimes the father, the responsibilities for the health, safety and education of the children falls on one person. In some cases, this leads to more sharing of power and responsibility between

Direct democracy at Summerhill School. Does everyone have a vote in your family or school?

25

Dad-Parent Families 21.5%

Mum-Parent Families 78.5%

Percentage of one-parent families which have a man or woman as head of the household, 1981

the adult and the children. Often the older children have to take a large part in looking after younger children and they may be included in decisions which have to be made concerning the welfare and future of the family.

In a few cases everyone in a family does what they want to do, when they want to do it. This may lead to conflict and disorder in the household. In a situation of near **anarchy**, such as this, where rules are not made, there are no sanctions (restraints) applied and power rests with each individual, then differences have to be resolved through discussion and compromise or else the family will break up, because what one member wants to do conflicts with others.

The home

One of the resources which members of a family usually have is the place where they live together. The allocation of space within a house or flat may reflect the distribution of power between members of the family:

- Often children have no space of their own, but share all the rooms they use with other people. They may share their bedrooms with brothers or sisters and the living room with everybody.
- The mother is often responsible for cleaning and maintaining all of the home, but usually has no space to herself, except perhaps the kitchen. Even the kitchen is

only her space in order to provide a service to the rest of the family.
- The father may have a space of his own. In some homes this may be a study or a garage or a garden shed, where, in some cases, others are not encouraged to go unless invited by him. The father's space may be a particular chair in which he always sits and which others move out of if he wants to sit down.

Families have several resources:

- space
- money
- knowledge
- time
- experience

The conflicts and arguments about how these are allocated between members of the family can be described as political discussions.

Politics outside the family

Society is reflected in the family

The type of patriarchal nuclear family we have already described is more likely to exist in a society where men are powerful outside the family, at work and in government, and have status in society. This is reflected in the organization of the family. The woman's work (child-rearing and maintaining the home and members of the family) is not paid and often not valued as highly as paid work outside the home. The man has more status and power both within the family and outside. Even in the symmetrical family, where the husband and wife share power more evenly, it is still likely that the man has higher status and more power outside the family. Most western industrialized societies are organized in this way and family organization often reflects the pattern of patriarchy.

Industry

In societies which are not industrialized, but are based on

Why do you think most company directors are men?

26

Why do you think most trade union leaders are men?

agriculture, or hunting and gathering, the family is an economic unit of production. That is, the family is like a small factory providing goods such as food, shelter and clothing that it needs for its members. All members of the family are important for the survival of each.

In industrialized societies families are not a unit of production. Adults are likely to be wage earners, working in shops, offices or factories, rather than with other members of

their family in the home to produce the things they need themselves. It is argued that as work has become more specialized, so have the functions of the family. Families in Britain no longer provide all the education, health services and welfare that their members need. There are other agencies such as schools, hospitals and social workers which have taken over such roles.

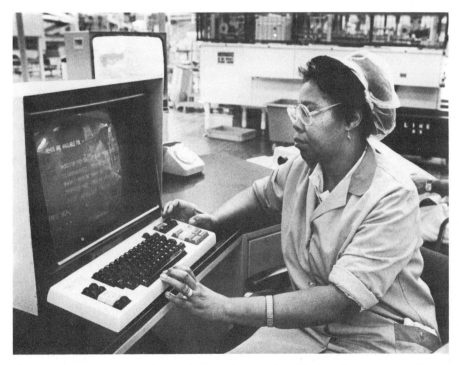

More women are using new technology in the workplace. Does this mean that these jobs will become low status with low pay?

Class

The family in Britain has become more isolated and home-centred. Nevertheless, there are still variations within Britain. Class differences in society are reflected in different patterns of family life in working-class homes and middle-class homes. It is more likely that in areas of poverty where welfare services cannot cope, members of the extended family will help out to provide support and care. In very wealthy families too extended relations are important in providing places in schools, jobs, marriage partners and homes through the network of family connections.

> **For example,** in Britain the royal family's extended relations are very important in providing status (which they do not have to achieve through work, but are ascribed at birth) and in ensuring that wealth is passed on from older members of the extended family to younger ones.

The family as a preparation for life

Children

The family is one group which prepares children for their adult lives. Parents teach children how to behave, what to believe and how to fit into their group in society. Children do not always accept what their family teaches them, but they do learn lessons, often by accident.

> **For example,** children are often expected to obey their parents without questioning them about why they should 'do as they are told' or about who gave their parents the right to tell them what to do. This kind of obedience to authority may produce people who, in later life, will obey rules and orders without questioning them.

Women

The role of women in the family is also reflected in their roles in wider society. In western industrial societies women are an important source of unpaid labour. They provide services in the home without which men would not be able to go out to work and keep industry productive. Many mothers, sisters and wives cook and clean up for men so that their sons, brothers and husbands can go out to work. In paid employment they are likely to be in some kind of service work, often related to the work they do in the home, perhaps as a teacher, cleaner, social worker, secretary or shop assistant, where, in general, they do not earn as much money as men, nor have such high status.

Background to the family in Britain

While the family in some form or other seems to be present in most societies it is not present in a single unchanging form. We have already seen that the modern image of a working father supporting a wife and children is not typical of the majority of families in Britain. Families and the ways in which they are organized vary within a particular society and over time. There is no reason to suppose that they will not continue to change in the future. Why families change and how changes affect the distribution of power and resources within families are important questions. We can learn some of the reasons for changes in family organization from a brief look at the changes in Britain since the sixteenth century.

Open families (sixteenth century)

In the early sixteenth century, families in all sections of society were characterized by:

- openness
- links with many distant relatives
- patriarchy
- the power of the eldest male

The eldest male was important in property ownership. Many people owned some property, even if it was only a small piece of land, and this was passed on from the father to the eldest son. In rich families, marriages were usually arranged on the basis of whether they would increase the wealth and power of the two families. The bride and groom were far from the first people to be consulted about marriage arrangements. The eldest son was the most important person in the family to find a suitable wife for, because he would inherit the land and property from his father and pass it on to his son. Younger sons and especially daughters were often unwanted because they were not an asset to the family but a drain on family resources.

There was often little importance placed on emotional ties between husbands and wives or even parents and children. The high death rate made marriages short and many children died soon after birth, so it did not pay to become too emotionally involved in each other's lives. The father and husband was the most important person in a family in all social classes, particularly the highest, and wives and children were

often completely **subordinate** to him.

> **For example,** in the early part of the next century, W Whately wrote, 'If ever thou purpose to be a good wife, and to live comfortably, set down this with thyself: mine husband is my superior, my better; he hath authority and rule over me; nature hath given it to him. . . . God hath given it to him.'
>
> From *The Bride Bush*, quoted in *The Family, Sex and Marriage in England, 1500–1800* by Lawrence Stone.

Smaller nuclear families (seventeenth century)

From about the beginning of the seventeenth century, the openness of families and their ties to distant relatives were declining, and the smaller nuclear family was becoming a more important centre for attention. With this shift the power of the male head of household increased further; since his empire was smaller, he could exert more influence and control over members of the family.

Church support

The new Protestant church, which was a powerful influence on people's thoughts and beliefs, supported the idea that the father and husband was almost all-powerful in his family. Women and children often accepted this position because of the strength of religious beliefs. So the male head of a household could become a kind of **despot** in the family, a position accepted by most men and women. This belief in the authority of the head of the establishment was mirrored in the wider society by the complete acceptance of the power of the king or queen over all subjects.

A wealthy Victorian extended family

Discipline

In middle-class families parents were extremely strict with children, often beating them into submission. This early training ensured that they would accept the decisions of their fathers later, particularly in two important areas of their lives:

- the occupations of their sons
- the marriage partners of their sons and daughters

The system of arranged marriages lasted longest in the wealthiest families, where economic and political ties were most important because there was more to be lost or gained. It is possible to see traces of arrangements over suitable brides and grooms still in the royal family in Britain.

In the poorest homes of the lower social classes the father was, again, the head of the household and the person to be obeyed by children, until they left home between the ages of ten and seventeen. Then they would come under the authority of a new master as an apprentice or domestic servant.

Women, at all levels of society, were subordinate to the authority of their husbands and fathers.

The media presented this as a fairy-tale wedding. Why was it important for a suitable bride to be found?

The eighteenth century

The broader political context of the family in Britain changed throughout the eighteenth century in response to changing economic and religous forces:

- The spread of industrialization meant that there was more wealth and more people shared it.

- This included women as well as men, and new laws were passed which enabled women to keep some of their own property or belongings when they married.

- The religious grip on society was lessened by scienific advances which helped to explain the world, so that it was more easily understood and some natural forces could be controlled. The world was no longer such a mystery, understandable only by God.

- These changes brought a greater degree of freedom for women in the family.

- Movements at this time to abolish slavery, reform prisons and improve the treatment of the mentally sick were accompanied by a more permissive attitude to children and their upbringing. Harsh beatings of children were no longer tolerated by the more enlightened sections of society.

The nineteenth and twentieth centuries

The first half of the nineteenth century saw a return to the authority of the father and strict child-rearing practices. This is probably because of general fears that the industrial poor might rise up and a revolution could take place. A return to

Drawing up a marriage contract between two wealthy families in the eighteenth century. Why was this necessary?

strictness and patriarchy was one way of preventing this.

Working women

From the middle of the nineteenth century and through the twentieth century, we can see a move away from such unequal relations between women and men and such harsh child rearing. This move has been greatest since the beginning of the First World War. During the First and Second World Wars (1914–18 and 1939–45), women took over many of the jobs in industry and farming which had previously been done mainly by men. However, after the Second World War many nurseries and day-care facilities for children were closed, men returned from war to paid jobs and women to the home. Nevertheless, it had been seen that women could take responsibilities

outside the home and many fought to defend that right.

Feminism

During the late 1960s, feminist writers in the United States and Britain began to criticize what they saw as male domination of both paid work and family life.

* They argued for a change in the patriarchal organization of families, so that men and women did not have to conform to stereotyped roles in which the women looked after the house and children while the men went out to work. The 1960s and '70s were times of relatively full employment, so there were opportunities outside the home for women to find work, and by the end of the 1970s women made up over 40 per cent of the workforce

in Britain. In many cases they were doing two jobs; one outside the home for which they were paid, and another at home doing housework and maintaining the family.

* Feminists began to argue for changes in the organization of work so that women could have children and a paid job, and men could take a greater part in child care and housework. Other demands which could change the ways in which work and families are organized are:
  – nursery provision
  – job sharing
  – equal pay
  – better promotion prospects for women
  – longer leave at the birth of a child for mothers and fathers.

Government response

The Government responded to pressure from women for changes and improvements in conditions of employment:

* They introduced the Equal Pay Act in 1970 and the Sex Discrimination Act in 1975.
* The Labour party created a post for an MP to speak on women's affairs.
* In France the Government created a **Cabinet** position for an MP with responsibility for women's rights.

Effects of unemployment and recession

The late 1970s and the beginning of the 1980s have been a time of rising unemployment and economic recession. This has affected women at work more severely than men:

Why did women do this sort of work during the Second World War? Why have things changed?

In this play-centre the children are safe and well cared for. Why is it important that child-care facilities are easily and cheaply available at work?

- Women have lost jobs at twice the rate of men, and black women at twice the rate of white women.
- Women's wages have fallen further and further behind those of

men, despite the Equal Pay Act. It is being argued by some that the economic conditions of the late twentieth century, with high and possibly permanent

unemployment, mean that the gains won so far by women will be lost.

- As unemployment rises women are being forced back into the home, where child rearing and cleaning replace paid employment.
- This decreases the need for welfare services to care for the young and elderly dependents, because wives, mothers and daughters can do it for nothing, leaving men to compete for paid employment.

For example, at home, women do nearly 80 per cent of household chores whether or not they go out to work.

This may mean the extended family ties will be strengthened once more, especially in the working-class families most affected by the economic climate. It may mean a radically different form of family organization will emerge which will recognize the important roles men and women have in child rearing, so that part-time work, job sharing and time off to bring up very small children will become a normal part of our lives.

Alternatives, the future, and you

Alternatives to the image of the traditional British family of one man, one woman and their children living together, already exist:

- In some cases women have chosen to reject the power of men in their lives as far as they are able, by bringing up children as women alone or with other women.
- In other cases people have chosen to share power more equally between the adults in a community or family. Some communes are organized so that men and women share all the roles in relation to child rearing, housekeeping and productive labour. Money is pooled so that

Who should do the housework? What people thought and what they did in 1984. (Some categories don't add up to 100 per cent because of non response/'don't knows'.)

Can women bring up children without men?

power within families we are also affecting wider social processes and politics.

1 Do you think it is a good idea for one person in a family to make all the major decisions?

2 What difficulties are there in involving all members of a family in the major decisions?

3 Are the children in your household involved in decision-making about such things as where to go on holiday, what to eat for dinner, and whether to move house or not? What can this kind of involvement teach people?

4 Who does the housework in your family? Why? How could it be different?

5 • Conduct a survey amongst your class to find out what kinds of households people live in and how work is divided between the people who live together.
   • Record your findings in graphic form.
   • What conclusions can you draw from your findings?

6 Draw a floor plan of your house or flat. Allocate each member of the household a colour – this is the key. Shade in the plan according to who controls the space in particular rooms or parts of the building. Think about what you mean by 'control' before you start. Does this show you anything about who has power in your household?

7 Imagine you want to go on a camping holiday abroad with two friends your own age but your parent(s) don't want you to go. Write down a list of arguments you could use to convince your parent(s) that you can go. Opposite this list write down all the counter-arguments you think a parent would use to stop you going.

one person does not dominate decisions or resources within the household.

Many people do not actively and consciously choose how they live with others, or how they raise their children if they choose to have them. Their lives are to some extent influenced and controlled by the dominant norms and values of their society. Certainly, no-one can vote on the identity of their parents or choose the type of household which they grow up in. When people reach adulthood they are in a better position to choose, and they do not have to fit in passively with what is expected of them. People choose to marry or not, to live alone or with other people of the same or opposite sex, to have children or not, and all for a variety of reasons. Emotional needs, financial reasons, security or an escape from parents and one's first experiences of family life are some of these reasons. The politics of the family often have to be confronted and resolved when these choices are made.

Summary

Politics within families vary considerably, between social classes and ethnic groups and throughout history. The way families and households are formed is usually a matter of convention (the way things have always been done): falling in love, getting pregnant, arranged partners or forming a collective. Whatever the form or the internal politics, all families are part of the social, religious and economic society in which they exist. When we try to change the nature of relationships and distribution of

5 · The politics of racism

What is race?

In Britain race differences and differences between people according to their colour have come to mean the same in people's minds. This confusion has led to the idea that biological and physical characteristics are important because they can be associated with social differences. In fact even the physical differences between peoples are often blurred and there is no evidence to prove that physical differences produce social differences.

Race has been used as the basis of scientific theories to explain differences in intelligence, attitudes and beliefs between groups of people. In particular, it has been used to justify the superiority of 'white' people and the inferiority of 'black' people whether Afro-Caribbean, Asian or African. So the term 'race' is not just a neutral biological term to describe appearances, but a political one which promotes inequality and the power of one group over another. A more useful term to describe peoples' different life styles, attitudes, values and beliefs is <u>ethnicity</u> or ethnic background. This term recognizes the differences between groups of people according to their <u>cultures</u> and not in terms of colour or other biological traits.

Racism

You have all heard racist remarks, slogans or 'jokes'. They usually refer to a person, often black or Irish, as if that person and everyone in the ethnic group to which they belong has some particular characteristic, which means they should be treated differently and as inferior.

An anti-racist rally – for many people it is important to demonstrate against racism

For example, jokes about the Irish usually assume that all Irish people are stupid and that they are stupid because they are Irish.

Racism is the belief that people can be grouped and classified differently according to their colour, or where they come from, and that they should be treated differently and have different rights according to their race! Racism demonstrates the power of one group over another. This power can be expressed in a variety of ways:

- Individuals can treat others as inferior or as objects of ridicule because of their race.
- Institutions such as the mass media, employment, or schooling can express and reinforce racist attitudes.

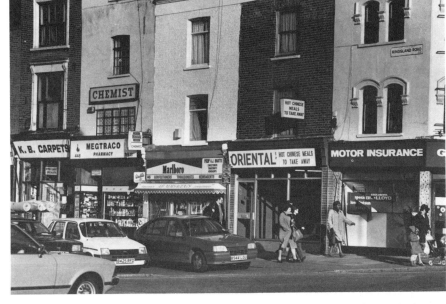

Why do you think that Chinese communities in Britain are less vulnerable to racist attacks than some other ethnic minority groups?

The media

- One view of the media is that television programmes, newspaper articles and magazines merely *reflect* the interests and views of the majority of the population.

- Another approach is to argue that the mass media are in a very powerful position in Britain to *influence* people's attitudes and to shape the way people think, and that they do not reflect like a mirror all views and interests, but mainly those of a small section of the population.

'I thought you said this was a quiet beach'. Stereotypes are often used in racist jokes and cartoons such as this one

Influencing or reflecting?

Television

Television can encourage negative attitudes towards ethnic minority groups in Britain. The use of stereotypes in television programmes can be seen as reinforcing and strengthening false images of ethnic groups. Some comedy programmes ridicule the differences between people and trade on myths and fears about 'foreigners'.

Books

In children's story books there have been examples of 'sambo' and 'golliwogs' who are unhappy because they are black. Many of these books were written a long time ago, but some are still being reprinted. However, more children's books are being written which include children from different cultural backgrounds and show them positively, as proud to be black and to have their own cultural identity.

Newspapers

In newspaper reports, headlines may give misleading ideas. In July 1970, a *Daily Express* headline read 'Police find 40 Indians in Black Hole; on the same day the *Daily Mail* headline was '40 Indians Invade', and the following day the *Sun* said 'The Invaders'. Whatever the newspapers meant by their headlines the message was clear: illegal immigrants were invading the country and were a threat and a danger. At about the same time a cartoon appeared in the *Mirror* in which a young couple were shown on a beach (see above). One of them is saying 'I thought you said this was a quiet beach', while the beach is being overrun by people wearing turbans, riding elephants, charming snakes and carrying beds of nails. These stereotypes of Asian culture were used to exaggerate the differences between Asian people and the white British population, and to ridicule these differences.

Newspaper headlines may also simplify events so much that what actually happened is lost.

> **For example,** during the riots in Brixton and Toxteth in the summer of 1981, headlines such as 'Black Day in Brixton' were used to suggest that the trouble was caused by and involved black youths only, when in fact black and white youths were involved in the street battles with police.

An example of reporting

An important area in which the media have been involved in reporting has been over immigration and especially the numbers of black immigrants entering Britain. In 1968 Enoch Powell was widely reported for his suggestion that there should be a total ban on black immigration

---

1,000 on rampage in Moss Side—fresh looting 'coordinated'

(Guardian, *9 July 1981*)

Police defend decision to launch 3am searches

(Guardian, *16 July 1981*)

THE RIOT CONSPIRACY

This was carefully planned guerilla warfare . . . and London accents were heard in Moss Side.

(New Standard, *9 July 1981*)

REVENGE OF THE MOB

About 50 Black people surrounded civil servants Mr Robert Morris and Mr Andrew Crook in Railton Road. One Black man shouted: 'This is war, man.'

(New Standard, *16 July 1981*)

These headlines are from two newspapers' accounts of the same events. What impression of the events does each newspaper give its readers?

Population changes and expected migration, 1901–2011

to Britain and possible repatriation, (that is, sending people back to their supposed country of origin). Enoch Powell became a 'media expert' on race and immigration. He was in a very powerful position, as a Member of Parliament, to make his views heard and to make them acceptable. The fact that the total number of people leaving the country has been greater in every year since the beginning of the century than the number entering (except for a few years in the 1930s and between 1958 and 1963) was lost in newspaper reports.

For example, look at how news is selected:

'The events were the publication on 10 March 1970 of the Registrar General's returns which showed that the birth rate among immigrants was higher than the national average, and the announcement by the Home Secretary that the rate of immigration was decreasing and that the number for the previous quarter was the lowest on record. Our comparisons are of the coverage of the events on 10 March and 15 March respectively, the days on which the news was first carried.

Seven of the eight dailies carried the birth figures, five of them on the front page. Only four carried the news about the reduction in immigration, only one of these on the front page ... Altogether there was about five times as much news-space given to the birth figures, and reactions to them as to the immigration figures ...'

From *The Mass Media and Racial Conflict* by Paul Hartman and Charles Husband.

The main emphasis of television and newspaper coverage, as well as research work, was that the race and numbers of the immigrant population was the problem and not the racism of the white society.

Power and influence

We can see from these examples the power and influence of the mass media to shape our attitudes and ideas.

- Not all news items are treated with the same seriousness and some views are not reported at all. Alternative ways of understanding situations might be ignored so that a dominant view becomes accepted. This is a conflict view of the role of the media.

- People who hold a consensus view would argue that everyone has the opportunity to make their views heard and to have them accepted.

Not all groups of people have the same amount of choice or power over their own lives. Some can choose what sort of job to do, others are not able to get a job at all or have to take whatever they are offered. Some can choose where to live and others are forced to live in areas of high unemployment or in unsatisfactory accommodation. In the following sections we will consider the relative powerlessness of ethnic minority groups in Britain to take control over their own lives in the areas of employment, housing and education. It should be clear that this relative powerlessness is not because of inborn differences, but because of widespread racism in British society.

Employment

Research by **PEP** in 1974 found that discrimination against black workers was widespread.

For example, Asian and West Indian men were found to suffer discrimination in at least 46 per cent of their applications for semiskilled and unskilled work. They also found it difficult to gain professional and managerial jobs: according to the report 79 per cent of white men with degree standard qualifications were in professional or managerial jobs, while only 33 per cent of similarly qualified black men were in such jobs.

Why do many small businesses employ women in sweat shops like this shoe factory?

Percentage of workers in professional and managerial work, 1982

Men

22%

7%

14%

key ☐ Whites ▨ Afro-Caribbeans ◼ Asians

Women

9%

1%

7%

Professional and managerial jobs have high status and high pay. Who is most likely to do them?

So a large proportion of black workers are forced to take jobs for which they are over-qualified. This is clearly a restriction on their choice, their freedom and their ability to control their own lives.

Research by **CRE** in 1978 in Lewisham ('Looking for work – black and white school leavers in Lewisham') found that black school leavers had to try more methods of finding work than their white peers.

> **For example,** the report claims that 'The young blacks we interviewed were looking for jobs just as hard as their white peers, but were still being markedly less successful'.
> 'Black teenagers are finding themselves at the absolute end of the jobs queue. A South London study of youth unemployment found that 70% of black girls had no job since leaving school as compared to 20% of white girls, 30% of white boys and 40% of black boys. "Sometimes the discrimination is quite obvious, and as employment opportunities tighten, it is getting worse," said Isadore Dunkley Joy, a black teenager on a job training scheme in North Kensington, who found that whenever she went for an interview she was always asked "Have you any criminal convictions?". Joy had come to accept this as normal procedure and was surprised to find that her white friends were never asked the same question.'
> From CIS report *Women in the Eighties*.

Not having a job affects many areas of people's lives in terms of the way they see themselves, how others see

Percentage of school-leavers unemployed, according to race and sex in 1978 (CRE)

them and, not least, how much money they have to spend. All of these are related to the relative powerlessness of the unemployed.

Great Britain		Ethnic group				All ethnic groups
		White	West Indian or Guyanese	Indian/ Pakistani/ Bangladeshi	Other	
Males of working age (i.e. aged 16 and over)						
• Economically active (i.e. working or seeking work)		88.2%	84.7%	82.6%	69.2%	87.7%
• Economically inactive (i.e. out of work)		11.8%	15.3%	17.4%	30.8%	12.3%
	Total (in thousands)	100% 16 281	100% 178	100% 409	100% 212	100% 17 327
Females of working age (i.e. aged 16 and over)						
• Economically active (i.e. working or seeking work)		66.0%	70.6%	45.5%	57.7%	65.4%
• Economically inactive (i.e. out of work)		34.0%	29.4%	54.5%	42.3%	34.6%
	Total (in thousands)	100% 14 763	100% 198	100% 349	100% 175	100% 15 716

Economic status by ethnic group, 1984

Why are people forced to live here?

Housing

A **GLC** survey in 1976 stated that 'non-whites secure less desirable accommodation than whites'.

> **For example,** they are more likely to be in flats rather than houses (92 per cent compared with 72 per cent), in older rather than more modern property (45 per cent in pre-1945 dwellings compared with 25 per cent), and on the higher floor of flats (38 per cent on the third floor or above compared with 27 per cent).

Council housing is not always available, especially to immigrants, black or white, who may not have lived in the borough long enough. There is some evidence that there has been a decrease in the discrimination against black people in buying houses, but some are still discriminated against when they go for rented accommodation in the private sector.

Discrimination on the grounds of colour, combined with low incomes, makes it difficult for some black people to find suitable accommodation.

Education

- Research by the National Child Development Study found that in general pupils of Irish and West Indian families scored below the average for all pupils in mathematics tests.

- Other research has shown that even though pupils from West Indian families are more likely to stay on at school after the fifth year, fewer have been entered for examinations, and those who have been, tend to have been entered for CSE rather than O level examinations.

- Several pieces of research have pointed to the higher school success of West Indian girls than that of West Indian boys, and to the higher levels of attainment of pupils from Asian families than all other ethnic groups.

> **For example,** according to the Rampton Committee, between 1978 and 1979 the proportions of school students going to university or polytechnic to study for a degree were: 5 per cent for students from Asian families, 1 per cent for those from West Indian families and 4 per cent for all other school leavers.

All of the research indicates that black students from West Indian families are underachieving in British schools.

- One explanation for this has been that many black children do not expect to do well in school and that many teachers have low expectations of them.
- Another explanation is that black pupils are often from working-class homes and all working-class children do less well than their middle-class peers in the education system.
- A further reason is that schools are mainly run by white, middle-class teachers and administrators, so that white, middle-class pupils tend to be at an advantage. The culture and home background of Asian pupils is more likely to fit into that middle-class school ethos than that of Afro-Caribbean pupils.

Whatever the explanation, low achievement in schools leads to less choice about jobs, possibly low income and less control over ones own life.

Background to immigration in Britain

Britain's colonial past helps to explain why many immigrants came to Britain and why racist attitudes exist towards them.

Nineteenth century emigrants

Ireland

England's earliest overseas colony was Ireland. From the twelfth century Irish people often moved to England to settle in the ports on the west coast, like Liverpool and Bristol. The Irish are the largest immigrant group in Britain today.

> **For example,** in 1860 Charles Kingsley wrote this:
>
> 'But I am haunted by the human chimpanzees I saw along that hundred miles of horrible country. I don't believe they are our fault. I believe there are not only many more of them than of old, but that they are happier, better, more comfortably fed and lodged under our rule than they ever were. But to see white chimpanzees is dreadful; if they were black, one would not feel it so much, but their skins, except where tanned by exposure, are as white as ours.'
>
> He was describing his visit to Ireland.

The slave trade

In the sixteenth century, sea traders began to bring slaves from West Africa to sell in England and later to sell in the West Indies, where Spanish settlers bought them to work on the sugar cane and cotton plantations.

In the seventeenth century, England acquired Barbados and Jamaica as part of its Empire and bought slaves from West Africa to work on the plantations. Britain was the leading trader in slaves, using them to work in its own colonies and selling them to other European countries such as Spain and Portugal. To justify this taking and selling of people as if they were objects, traders and slave owners argued that the slaves were subhuman and therefore it did not matter how they were treated. They were seen to be natural slaves by white men, who viewed themselves as natural masters.

The slave trade was immensely profitable for Britain, but in 1833 slavery was abolished and slaves were set free in the British Empire.

In India, British influence began as early as 1600 when the East India Company began trading with and conquering India. India was very profitable for Britain as a source of raw materials and cheap labour, as well as providing a market for Britain's goods.

It was from this colonial past, when small numbers of white British officers and traders ordered and directed black workers, that ideas about white superiority and black inferiority emerged.

Unemployment

By the end of the nineteenth century there was rising unemployment in Britain and people were encouraged to emigrate to the colonies, mainly Canada, Australia, New Zealand and those in Africa. However, after the Second World War there was a labour shortage and so workers were encouraged to come to Britain from those colonies. Many, but not by any means all, black workers went into low-paid, unskilled work, because that was where the vacancies were. Low incomes and discrimination against them reinforced their inferior position and encouraged racist attitudes. These attitudes remain with us to some extent.

The role of the Government

Immigration Acts

Until 1962 people from the commonwealth countries and from the UK and colonies had the right to come and live in Britain. (This was because, in the past, Britain had accepted it as its right to dominate and colonize those countries.) In 1962 the first Commonwealth Immigration Act was passed.

- On the one hand it was argued that this Act was necessary to restrict the numbers of unskilled workers entering Britain when fewer were needed.
- A different view is that this Act effectively prevented, not unskilled workers, but black people coming into Britain, and established the idea that black immigrants were a problem and that there were too many.

When Britain had needed workers in the expanding factories in the 1950s, the Government and British firms had advertised for workers in the Caribbean, India and Pakistan. London Transport recruited drivers and conductors from the Caribbean, and the Health Service advertised for workers in the Caribbean, India and Pakistan. The British economy

False promises of good jobs, housing and prospects encouraged people to come to Britain from the Caribbean

depended at that time on immigrant workers to fill jobs that British people living in Britain either could not or would not do. The need for extra labour declined by the 1960s and 70s and so a series of Government Acts from 1962 until the 1971 Immigration Act were passed. These severely limited the number and types of people who could live and work in Britain.

> **For example,** in 1973 those entitled to enter and settle were:
>
> - 'Commonwealth citizens whose parents or grandparents were born in Britain. These people are called **patrials** and come mainly from countries such as Australia and Canada. Commonwealth citizens without a parent/grandparent born in Britain are called non-patrials and are subject to strict immigration control.
> - 'Wives, husbands, fiancé(e)s, children under 18 years and certain other dependants of commonwealth citizens who are already settled in Britain.
> - 'People who have UK passports and who have no other citizenship. These are mainly Asians in East Africa. Their entry is subject to a special voucher system, 5000 vouchers being given each year. In 1977 only 2032 of these were taken up, which suggests that there will be little more immigration of Asians from Africa.'
>
> From *Our People*, produced by Thames Television.

The three tier system

The 1981 Nationality Act introduced a three tier system of nationality:

- Full British citizenship is for patrial UK and commonwealth citizens.
- Citizenship of the British dependent territories is the category for residents of Hong Kong, Gibraltar etc, and does not carry automatic right of entry.
- British overseas citizenship is for non-patrial British people from former dependencies, and carries no right of entry into British territory.

British Governments, Conservative and Labour, have been applying stricter and stricter controls on who can live and work in Britain if they are black. Some critics of this immigration policy have argued that it is this in itself which has created a climate of racism in Britain, by treating immigrants from predominantly black countries

differently from those from mainly white countries. It is also argued that this has focused the argument on numbers of immigrants, rather than on the racism of the host population. The Government, the mass media and a sizeable proportion of the population of Britain all seemed to be in agreement in the 1960s and 70s that there was a need for laws to limit immigration.

Race relations

Other Government policies between 1965 and 1976 have been concerned to promote good race relations. There have been three Race Relations Acts, in 1965, 1968 and 1976. At present the law is intended to prevent discrimination in employment, housing and education and in the provision of goods, services and facilities, on the grounds of race or ethnic origin. The law covers *direct* discrimination (that is, less favourable treatment on grounds of colour, race, nationality, ethnic or national origins) as well as *indirect* discrimination (that is, conditions which apply to everyone but have an adverse effect on one or more racial minorities).

The Race Relations Acts have been introduced to improve the position of black people and all ethnic minority groups in Britain by making discrimination illegal in important areas. The Acts have had some success in preventing discriminatory practices, but we do not know the extent to which they have helped to

A Polish cultural centre and a Yiddish theatre: some communities have become more established in Britain than others. Why?

change people's attitudes. Some people claim that the Race Relations Acts and the local Councils for Racial Equality have removed the power of black community leaders to make more radical and far-reaching changes.

Ethnic community politics

At an informal level of support and mutual assistance, ethnic minority groups in Britain, like many other countries, rely on family and friends. Religious and social ties (including music, food) and many attitudes, practices and beliefs, draw people who share them together, so that self help within and between families is common and valuable as a means of support. At times when people feel threatened more formal, political groups emerge both to defend and promote their rights.

In Britain the Rastafarian movement combines religious belief in a black messiah with political ideals which explain the oppressed position of black people in British society, and offers those who follow an opportunity to change their position. The Black Workers' Movement aligns itself with the working class, black and white, and aims for radical change in the structure of British society.

Black teenagers and parents have established supplementary schools in some parts of Britain to provide the kind of education they want but feel is not offered in the mainstream school system. The Asian Youth Movement and other ethnic action groups have been formed to provide information about their history and culture, to support each other and to provide alternative explanations for their unequal position in British society. Their political successes so far have been limited.

One successful political action organized by a number of black people's groups was the campaign against **SUS**, the 1824 Vagrancy Act. This law allowed police to arrest a person without a warrant if they

Why is it important for black people to be better represented in Britain's local and national politics?

had reasonable suspicion that the person might be about to commit a crime. Young black people were more likely to be arrested on SUS than any other group of people. A major campaign to repeal the law was mounted by black people's organizations. They gained the support of the National Council of Civil Liberties and of the Labour and Liberal parties, and eventually the repeal of the law in 1981 by the Conservative Government.

Their action was successful in changing the law. This may have been because they focused on one goal and enlisted the support of a wide range of pressure groups and the political parties. They did secure a change in the law and this may present a model and a way forward for black people's politics over other issues.

Summary

We have considered racism in some institutions in Britain such as education, housing and employment. These are not the only areas in which black people experience racism. Just as sexism exists in language, images in the media and everyday practices, so does racism.

'There are certain routine practices, customs and procedures in our society whose consequence is that black people have poorer health, housing, education and life-chances than do the white majority, and less influence on the political and economic decisions which affect their lives. These practices and customs are maintained by relations and structures of power from which black people have been and are excluded. This web of discriminatory practices and procedures is what is meant by the term "institutional racism".'

(from Race, Sex and Class. A Policy for Equality; Race – ILEA.)

Racism is often unrecognized or denied. It is often unconscious and so not seen as a serious problem. However, as we have seen, black people experience racism in Britain and their experiences should affect the political activities of everyone. In terms of the politics of every-day-life this involves us in recognizing and combating our own racism as well as challenging that of others.

1 What is the difference between *ethnicity* and *race*?

2 What is meant by *racism*?

3 Why was it thought necessary in the 1950s to encourage people from the Caribbean and Asia to come to Britain?
Do you know any people who came to Britain about that time? Ask them why they came, what they expected to find when they arrived, if they were disappointed and what they miss.

4 Why was it thought necessary in the 1960s and 1970s to discourage people from the Caribbean and Asia from coming to Britain?

5 It is illegal to ride a motorbike without wearing a crash helmet. Some Sikhs have objected to this, as their religious customs require men to wear a turban, which makes wearing a crash helmet impossible. Do you think this law discriminates against Sikhs? Can you find any other examples of what you think is direct or indirect discrimination?

6 How can an understanding of the history of the slave trade and slavery help to explain attitudes in Britain today?

7 What can schools, students and staff, do to combat racism? Consider areas such as language, grafitti, attitudes, the content of lessons and anti-racist policies.

6 · The politics of the mass media

What are the mass media?

The mass media are all the ways of communicating the same message to a large number of people. They include:

- books, newspapers and magazines (printed communication)
- radio, records and audio-tapes (audio communication)
- cinema, television and video (audiovisual communication)

The mass media are an important political force in Britain and most parts of the world today. Almost all homes in Britain have a television set and a radio. The majority of the population see a daily paper. Most people rely on the television and the daily newspapers for information about what is going on in the world, and so it is on these two media that this Chapter will concentrate.

All newspaper articles and television programmes, whether they are fictional stories or factual documentaries, are constructed; that is to say they are made and built up by journalists, editors and programme makers. The process of making an article for a newspaper or a programme for television involves choices: selecting, rejecting and creating pieces to go into the final version. This process might be political in so far as the choices are made from a position of power and from particular view points.

News is selected, rejected and organized before it leaves this newsroom for the public

Political effects of the mass media

Some people would argue that television, in particular, has a very powerful *influence* on our ideas, attitudes, beliefs and even on our behaviour. Others would claim that television merely *reflects* the range of attitudes which already exist in society, and that people will choose to watch programmes which confirm their existing beliefs rather than those which challenge them. It is certainly the case that people tend to choose to read the daily paper which broadly corresponds with their political attitudes, rather than a paper with whose point of view they disagree.

The effects of the mass media on political attitudes are difficult to assess. They are not the only influence to which we are exposed. Families, friends and schools all contribute towards our attitudes and

beliefs. We do not passively absorb messages from the mass media or other influential agents. We are not blotting paper soaking up information and ideas, in amounts which can be measured later. We interpret what we see and hear and read: we

discuss it with other people, and digest it so that it fits in with other things we believe about ourselves and about society and with experiences we have had. The relationship between the mass media and their audiences is a complicated one. There are two main ways of looking at this relationship.

The liberal consensus view

From this point of view it is argued that the media expose people to a wide range of opinions. The public is then free to accept or reject these opinions as they wish.

Choice of newspapers

In Britain there are many daily newspapers and people choose which one to buy.

- If they want a paper which usually supports the Conservative party they can buy the *Daily Telegraph*, the *Daily Express* or the *Daily Mail*.
- If they want a paper which generally supports the policies of the Labour party they can buy the *Daily Mirror* or *The Guardian*.
- If people cannot find a newspaper which expresses their own views or that of a group to which they belong, they can set up their own newspaper. Of course not everyone can afford to set up their own newspaper, but the supporters of the liberal view argue that the freedom to do so exists and that is what is important.

People interpret what they see on TV according to their experience and the social groups to which they belong

Points of view

People who hold the liberal consensus view also argue that the public can make their views known:

- They can write letters to the newspapers, since most papers publish a selection of readers' letters, and occasionally longer pieces.
- Individuals or groups can make their voices heard on television access programmes such as Channel 4's *Opinion* and *Help* on ITV.

However, the letters to newspapers make up a small part of the total paper, and those published are a small number selected by the editor from all those sent in. Also access programmes are only a small proportion of the total output of television and are usually not on at peak viewing times.

Balanced coverage

In television broadcasting, the Broadcasting Act insists that the independent television companies provide a 'balance of information, education and entertainment . . . and so far as possible, accuracy in news, impartiality in matters of controversy, and the maintenance of good taste'. The BBC is also expected to present a balance of information, education and entertainment and within that a balance of opinions. So television is expected to be fair to all those involved in a dispute and not to influence the audience by giving more time or credibility to one side against others. Those who hold the liberal consensus view argue that a wide range of opinions is expressed, none of which is more favoured than others.

The public has control

A final argument in support of this view is that the public can control the media:

- by switching off their television sets
- by not buying a newspaper with which they disagree

The effect of large numbers of people not watching a programme or

BRITAIN'S NATIONAL NEWSPAPERS

Populars		Circulation in thousands	
Daily	Owner	1975	1985
Sun	Rupert Murdoch	3,446	4,125
Daily Mirror	Robert Maxwell	3,968	3,033
Daily Express	United Newspapers	2,822	1,902
Daily Mail	Associated Newspapers	1,726	1,815
Daily Star	United Newspapers	(began 1978)	1,455
Sunday			
News of the World	Rupert Murdoch	5,479	5,103
Sunday Mirror	Robert Maxwell	4,251	3,009
Sunday People	Robert Maxwell	4,188	2,962
Sunday Express	United Newspapers	3,715	2,449
Mail on Sunday	Associated Newspapers	(began 1982)	1,631

TIME Chart by Joe Lertola

Qualities			1975	1985
Daily	Owner		1,331	1,202
Daily Telegraph	Conrad Black		319	487
Guardian	Guardian Newspapers		319	478
Times	Rupert Murdoch		181	234
Financial Times	Pearson P.L.C.			
Sunday			1,380	1,251
Sunday Times	Rupert Murdoch		752	736
Sunday Telegraph	Conrad Black		730	686
Observer	Tiny Rowland			

Although there is a wide choice of national daily newspapers, they do not necessarily present a wide range of views not buying a newspaper forces those particular media controllers to change or to go out of business. This idea that the media respond to audiences and to public opinion is important to the liberal consensus view.

The conflict view

A different way of seeing the relationship between the mass media and the public is put forward by those who support a conflict view. From this position it is argued that the media serve to justify major differences in society, especially differences in wealth, income and status.

Cover up

The conflicts in our society between rich and poor, bosses and workers, men and women, or between government and the governed, are made to seem natural and inevitable (as if this is the *only* way it could be) in the ways they are described by television and newspapers. In some cases the conflicts and differences between groups in society are covered up so that the real causes of conflict are not revealed. From this view the mass media serve to maintain the **status quo**, that is, keeping things as they are. So it is said to be biased in favour of keeping society as it is. Supporters of this view would argue that far from presenting a wide range of opinions, the mass media are inclined to give more time and importance to the opinions of those who form part of the ruling class, such as politicians, professional people, employers etc.

Bias

The Glasgow University Media Group studied television coverage of news items in 1976 and claimed that the language, the photographs and the approach of news reporters was

biased in favour of employers and to the disadvantage of workers or employees.

> **For example,** in **industrial disputes** the employers made 'offers' and 'pleas' while the workers made 'threats' and 'demands'. The reasons for the industrial conflict were often not explained fully, if at all, in television news reports. Disputes were described as the 'dustcart drivers' dispute' or the 'civil servants' dispute', without mentioning the employers or the Government. In this way it was made to seem as if the conflict was caused solely by the workers, when it might have been that the employers contributed to the dispute by paying low wages, making workers redundant or imposing longer hours.

The Glasgow University Media Group concluded that television news:

- is not presented in a balanced or impartial way
- only presents part of the story, neglecting some areas of opinion
- is undemocratic in the selection of who is seen as important enough to speak on the television news

Ownership and control of the media

Ownership of a resource can and often does mean control over one's own life and the lives of others. In the case of the mass media the ownership of newspapers or television broadcasting facilities can mean power to influence the ideas, attitudes and beliefs of their audiences. So it is worth noting who owns television broadcasting and newspapers if we want to see who has power and how much they have. The extent of their power and how much they have will depend on how much control owners have. Sometimes controllers of the media are not the same as the owners.

Television

The BBC

The BBC is owned by the State. It is a government controlled organization, rather like a

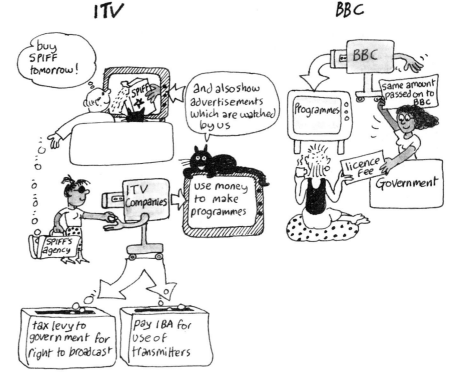

How television programmes are paid for

'Subliminal' Advertising	**8**	No television advertisement may include any technical device which, by using images of very brief duration or by any other means, exploits the possibility of conveying a message to, or otherwise influencing the minds of, members of an audience without their being aware, or fully aware, of what has been done.
Politics, Industrial and Public Controversy	**9**	No advertisement may be inserted by or on behalf of any body, the objects whereof are wholly or mainly of a political nature, and no advertisement may be directed towards any political end. No advertisement may have any relation to any industrial dispute. No advertisement may show partiality as respects matters of political or industrial controversy or relating to current public policy.
Religion	**10**	No advertisement may be inserted by or on behalf of any body, the objects of which are wholly or mainly of a religious nature, and no advertisement may be directed towards any religious end.
Charities	**11**	No advertisement may give publicity to the needs or objects of any association or organisation conducted for charitable or benevolent purposes.
*This Act does not extend to Northern Ireland		*(This does not preclude advertisements which are confined to the giving of necessary details of flag days, fêtes, lotteries permitted under the Lotteries and Amusements Act 1976*, other events organised by such associations or organisations or publications of general interest.)*
Good Taste	**12**	No advertisement should offend against good taste or decency or be offensive to public feeling.

Some of the Independent Broadcasting Act guidelines which regulate advertising on ITV and Channel 4

nationalized industry such as steel, coal, gas and electricity, which do not have to make profits, but are essential services. It is regulated by a Board of Governors who are twelve people appointed by the Government. The governors are not politicians, but they are political appointments. The Prime Minister selects people from a list of possible candidates. The ones chosen might not have any particular party political views and they might not agree with the party in government, but they are considered to be able to do the job.

The money to produce BBC programmes comes from collecting licence fees. Everyone who owns a television set must have a licence by law. The Post Office, another government organization, collects the television licence money and passes it on to the BBC, who then use it to pay for programme directors, producers, actors, equipment, etc.

In theory, every adult who owns a television set owns part of the BBC, because they all help to pay for it and they elect the government that appoints the governors. In practice, this ownership is so remote and distant from the production of the programmes that it is often the programme producers who have most control. These are the professionals who run the BBC. However, the licence given to the BBC to allow them to broadcast demands that the programmes do not take sides in any controversial matter, or edit material so that only one view is presented.

ITV

ITV is a group of privately owned companies including Anglia, London Weekend, Central and Thames. There are about fifteen such independent television companies. Each one makes programmes for television and pays rental every year to the Independent Broadcasting Authority, which owns the transmitting stations and regulates the activities of the private television companies. A Board of Members, chosen by the Government, constitutes a similar body to the BBC's Board of Governors. Through the **IBA** the State has some control over ITV and Channel 4.

The money to make programmes for ITV comes from the companies that advertise their products on television. The television companies sell time to businesses that want to advertise their products and are prepared to spend large sums of money to buy television time. Viewers who buy products advertised on television are paying indirectly for the programmes and the advertisements. It can be argued that if viewers do not buy products which are advertised on television then the programme-makers, or the product, will have to change or go out of business. In this way, it is said, the audience exerts control over what is shown on television. So independent television has to be successful at selling products and to do this the programmes have to appeal to people who have money to spend on buying the products advertised.

Television companies are not entirely free to show whatever programmes they want. The IBA states that ITV and Channel 4 must 'ensure that the programmes provide a proper balance of information, education and entertainment'. The

Television		Radio	
	£m		£m
BBC 1	223	Radio 1	12
BBC 2	116	Radio 2	26
Regional	47	Radio 3	25
		Radio 4	35
		Regional	25
		Local	18
Transmission	14	Transmission	8
Capital costs	59	Capital costs	27
Total	**459**	**Total**	**176**

How the BBC spent its money in 1983

advertising is also controlled by the Act, so that religious and educational programmes do not carry any advertisements, and some types of advertisements are not allowed.

> **For example,** advertisements are not allowed on TV for products which:
> - might be harmful (such as cigarettes)
> - might be considered offensive (such as pornographic magazines)
> - might not work (such as hair restorers)

Both the BBC and independent television channels are regulated by bodies appointed by the Government; their objectives, to provide a variety of types of programmes and avoid biased presentation, are the same; and they are both paid for by the viewers, either directly (BBC licences) or indirectly (advertising). While overall control rests with the Government, the immediate control of programmes is in the hands of programme-makers who want to attract audiences.

Newspapers

Background
Historically newspapers have been privately owned.

Newspapers are paid for by selling advertising space and by selling the paper

> **For example,** the *Daily Mail* was influenced by one of the early newspaper 'barons' or owners. Alfred Harmsworth, who later became Lord Northcliffe, founded the *Daily Mail* in 1896. He owned the paper and took a direct and personal interest in what it printed. He sacked journalists who wrote articles he did not like, and instructed them which issues and events to write about. His brother, Lord Rothermere, took over the ownership in 1922 and continued to sack editors and journalists with whom he disagreed, so that his own, personal views were often those published in the newspaper.

Newspaper owners such as these were often peers, always wealthy and were able to express their own views as they liked, while preventing anyone else criticizing them through their newspapers. Lord Beaverbrook, who owned the *Daily Express*, was the last of these newspaper barons when he died in 1965. Recently, another such newspaper owner has emerged, Rupert Murdoch, who owns the *Sun* and *The Times* and has been inclined to behave like the earlier newspaper owners in influencing the views expressed in his papers.

Who has the power?
It has become less and less

Who pays for this 'free' paper? How does that affect the news items which it carries?

acceptable to politicians and the public to allow such an obvious exercise of power to continue, especially when that power comes from inherited wealth. Throughout the twentieth century newspaper ownership has been concentrated into fewer but larger companies. News International, Trafalgar House, Reed International and Associated Newspapers now own the majority of all national, daily and Sunday newspapers printed in Britain.

- They also have other business interests in book publishing, the record and film industries and property.
- They are concerned with making money and therefore with selling as many copies of their newspaper as possible.
- They are not so interested in the content of the newspapers as the earlier newspaper proprietors were. Editors and journalists generally have more control over what the paper prints than they had in the past.

Where does the money come from?

The money to print a newspaper comes from two main sources:

- part comes from the people who buy the newspaper
- most comes from companies that pay to advertise in the newspaper

Newspapers have to attract advertisers in order to make money. Companies will not want to advertise in a newspaper if they think that not enough people buy that paper, or that the people who do buy it cannot afford their product.

> **For example,** in 1964 the *Daily Herald*, a national daily paper which supported the Labour party, was closed because it could not attract advertisers. Even though large numbers of working people bought the *Daily Herald*, the advertisers did not think that its readers could buy their products and so the newspaper was forced to close. It was replaced by the *Sun*, which did not support the Labour party only and so attracted a wider and more affluent working class readership. As a result advertisers supported it.

Advertisers can also influence what is printed in the newspaper articles.

> **For example,** the editor of the *City Press*, a financial paper, was unable to publish articles about the practices of Slater-Walker, a large company, because the paper needed the money which Slater-Walker paid them for advertising space. If they had printed an article which was critical of Slater-Walker, it might have prompted the company to stop buying advertising space from them, which would have put the paper in severe financial difficulties.

The Government also exerts some controls over newspapers. Journalists depend on government departments for information and press releases. These present the amount, the content and the timing of the information that the Government wants the public to know.

The mass media and the Government

Politicians, political parties and governments need the mass media in order to communicate with the electorate. They need to pass on information, and in a democracy they need to make their policies and practices sound attractive so that they will win votes in the next election. Newspapers and television play a vital role in the way information is passed on and in the ways political parties, politicians and their policies are presented to the public. The mass media have become part of the political process in modern Britain.

Television

The political link between government and television is not party political. However, the people chosen to oversee television are drawn from a small section of society and are mainly peers, wealthy businessmen or landowners. Nevertheless, television is not meant to present a more favourable view of one section of the population or of one political party. The regulations and laws which govern television broadcasting state that they must be balanced, impartial and independent of government.

Sometimes television is not independent of government.

> **For example,** during the conflict in the Falklands Islands in 1982, all news coverage was censored by the Ministry of Defence. After the Falklands war there were discussions about whether or not the Government should control the information available and censor views that disagreed with government actions.

Does this kind of political campaign, used during the 1983 General Election, pass on useful information to the voters? What purpose did it serve?

Extract from the Real Lives documentary. When is censorship in the 'national interest'?

Does this mean that the rest of the paper is for Guardian men?

In times when there is not a social or political crisis such as the Falklands war, television is supposed to be independent of government, but the governors of the BBC and the IBA are meant to act in the 'national interest'. This means that they sometimes refuse to show programmes which might threaten the national interest.

> **For example,** the IBA refused to broadcast a programme called *South of the Border*, which gave a view of Northern Ireland from some people in the Republic of Ireland. It was thought that the programme was not 'balanced' and it would not be in the national interest to show it.
>
> A similar thing happened in 1985 when the BBC documentary, *Real Lives*, was due to be shown. It was on Northern Ireland and some of the views of those interviewed were 'controversial'. The BBC stopped the programme from being shown. But there was a lot of protest and eventually it was screened.

Newspapers

On the whole newspapers in Britain are conservative in the sense that they generally support the status quo and do not advocate radical or dramatic changes in society.

The treatment of women in the newspapers is one example of how the press act as a conservative force to keep the popular image of women as inferior to men.

> **For example**
> * Most of the tabloids, or popular press, have a pin-up each day, which reinforces the view of women as attractive objects rather than people.
> * Very few of the newspapers report news made by women or of special interest to women, except on the 'Woman's Page', which is a small part of the total paper. The idea of a special page or section for women is offensive to many women who think that the whole paper should cater for them, not just a small part of it dealing with fashion and cookery. Women *and* men miss out when news is only presented from one point of view or only reflects some people's activities and concerns.

It is not surprising that most British newspapers support the Conservative party or are conservative in their coverage of events:

* They rely on attracting advertisers, selling newspapers and making money in order to survive in business.
* They have a close relationship to the business world and profit making, and so an interest in maintaining the structure and organization of society more or less as it is.

In one-party systems such as those of Communist countries like China, Cuba and the USSR, the press is usually controlled directly by the government. In these countries newspapers are an important part of government. The press is supposed to support and promote the aims of the government and not to criticize it. There is no attempt to be impartial or to offer various views on a particular event. It is argued by supporters of the Communist press that such aims in democracies are impossible to achieve. Western journalists, they say, report the news from their own biased, usually middle-class, point of

Disturbed by the tales of child-abuse which erupt into the headlines — and those which never become public — three Humberside women are trying to do something to eliminate them. MARGARET GREENFIELD reports

Traditionally-tailored shooting suit from Harrods personal tailoring department in Reid and Taylor's house tartan. Her shooting suit and hat, with a turn-of-the-century influence, are by Caroline Charles.

Dianne Core: "It leaves you with all sorts of hang-ups, not least a terrible, deep-seated anger."

DIANNE CORE relates rather better than most to the short, tragic and traumatic lives of Jasmine Beckford, Tyra Henry and Maria Colwell.

At the age of 40 she still carries the emotional scars inflicted by the physical abuse she suffered as a child at the hands of her father. Although these days the fear and pain that she experienced as a bewildered, battered and lonely six-year-old manifest themselves as nightmares.

"It is something you never get over, even if you are lucky enough to survive any lasting physical damage. It leaves you with all sorts of hang-ups,

Taming a nightmare

death, and I would much rather have 10 over-zealous housewives than one dead child," she said. So far as Dianne a former social worker is concerned it is

for some unaccountable reason, her father (who probably became deeply disturbed), vented his frustration and anger on her, with constant beatings,

Going festive in plaid

WHEN John Packer stages one of his biennial fashion spectaculars he believes in pushing the boat out. It is always the most extravagant of occasions and this year's show, in Edinburgh, promises to be no exception.

Held every two years to promote the luxury cloths produced by Reid and Taylor, the Scottish Borders mill of which he is managing director, the shows have become

Families and fashion – aren't men interested in these too?

---

view and then present it as unbiased fact, so that readers are deluded into accepting what they read as the truth. The Communist press presents the truth in the form of bias in favour of the Communist party. Because the Communist party, they claim, represents the wishes and ideas of the people then this bias is in the interests of the people.

Alternatives

Dutch Television

For example, in Holland no television company is allowed to make a profit, and each company has an openly political, social or religous aim. There are eight private television companies:

Company	Interest
NCRV	Protestant
KRO	Catholic
VARA	Socialist
VPRO	Progressive
AVRO	Conservative/Liberal
EO	Youth culture
VOO	Pop
TROS	Entertainment

Each company has a particular interest and bias, but not all of their programmes put over that message directly. In order to be able to

broadcast each company must provide a comprehensive range of programmes, which includes a variety of different items. The money for the television companies comes from licence fees and a few advertisements. A government organization watches over the companies and makes sure they conform to the broadcasting regulations.

Dutch viewers can choose between the type of bias they want, as long as

it is represented in the range of television companies. They can be sure that none of the programmes are made for commercial reasons, because no television company is allowed to make a profit. The Dutch argue that this system:

- enables more points of view to be expressed on television, giving viewers more choice than British viewers have (i.e. between BBC and ITV programmes);
- is more democratic than the

ПРОДОВОЛЬСТВЕННОЙ ПРОГРАММЫ

СОЦИАЛИСТИЧЕСКИЕ ОБЯЗАТЕЛЬСТВА

КОЛЛЕКТИВА ОРДЕНА ТРУДОВОГО КРАСНОГО ЗНАМЕНИ ЭКСПЕРИМЕНТАЛЬНО-ПОКАЗАТЕЛЬНОГО ПРОИЗВОДСТ- ВЕННОГО ОБЪЕДИНЕНИЯ РЫБНОЙ ПРОМЫШЛЕННОСТИ «БАЛЫКЧИ» ГОСРЫБХОЗА УЗБЕКСКОЙ ССР ПО УСКОРЕНИЮ НАУЧНО-ТЕХНИЧЕСКОГО ПРОГРЕССА И ПОВЫШЕНИЮ НА ЭТОЙ ОСНОВЕ ЭФФЕКТИВНОСТИ ПРОИЗВОДСТВА В ДВЕ- НАДЦАТОЙ ПЯТИЛЕТКЕ

Коллектив ордена Трудо- вого Красного Знамени экс- периментально - показатель- ного производственного объ- единения рыбной промыш- ленности «Балыкчи», руко- водствуясь решениями ап- рельского (1985 г.) Пленума

прирост производства обес- печить за счет повышения производительности труда.

Осуществить комплекс мер по повышению качества и расширению ассортимента рыбопродукции, увеличить

ного труда на 6 процентов, высвободить 65 рабочих.

От технического перево- оружения получить эконо- мический эффект не менее 500 тысяч рублей. Сэконо- мить 100 тысяч киловатт- часов электроэнергии и 160 тонн условного топлива. Снижать ежегодно себестои- мость выпускаемой продук- ции сверх задания на 0,5 процента.

Довести количество ук- рупненных комплексных хозрасчетных бригад с опла- той труда по конечным ре- зультатам до 90 процентов. Повысить квалификацию, обучить вторым профессиям не менее 250 рабочих.

Why do Soviet papers present the views of the Communist party?

British system. If any group can prove that they have a membership of at least 150 000 people they are allocated a certain number of hours in which to broadcast. In this way the companies with most members get most television time.

Community news

Television

Cable television has many advantages.

- Cables laid underground and going into homes could carry up to forty different television channels.
- Not only could these cables deliver pictures to television screens, they could also carry messages back from the television sets to the companies who produced the programme.
- This new technology of cable television could change the relationship between television and the public.
- Local television stations are possible, so that a community or a local area could own and control their own television broadcasts.
- Viewers could participate in local affairs, and be better informed about and involved in local politics.

However, the cost of placing the cables to make this possible is very high.

For example, in America, cable television is available at a cost, so that those who can afford better quality programmes and more variety are able to receive them.

Community television, which serves the needs of people, responds to them, and can be controlled directly by them requires a lot of money to set up. This is because the cables that carry the television pictures are very expensive to put in place. It seems likely that the money to develop cable television will come from business, rather than pressure groups, political parties or local communities.

If this is the case then cable television will be owned and controlled by businesses and will be money-making enterprises, rather than a means for encouraging and enabling local decision-making or participation in local and national politics. As such it will not be dramatically different from the style and content of television programmes which are already available on BBC and ITV.

Newspapers

What are community newspapers?

- There was an increase of them in the 1970s.
- They often rely on volunteer workers and little money.
- Their aims are to inform and educate their readers, usually about particular issues, either local or of concern to their readers.
- They are often openly political and critical of the existing state of affairs.
- A community newspaper can appeal to people living in a particular area, or to people with a similar cultural background or religious beliefs.

In the 1980s the TUC is talking about establishing a daily paper which will appeal to trade union members. Some women's groups have their own newsletter, housing estates run community papers and pressure groups such as **CND** often have a publication. One of the major problems for the development of these types of papers is the increasing cost of publishing.

A local community newspaper published in Britain

Eddie Shah has used new technology to produce his newspaper. How have people reacted to the loss of jobs this created?

used to avoid controlling or censoring images on television or in newspapers. But gaining access to television time and newspaper space is very expensive so this is not a freedom which everyone can exercise equally.

People can turn off their TV sets or refuse to buy a newspaper if they object to the contents. If enough people do this they might create a change in what is produced. However, their power to do this is limited if the owners of these media can still make money without them. Their only alternative is to set up their own newspaper or television company. This, of course, requires money. The politics of the mass media is closely connected to economics and the power of money.

The future of the mass media in Britain as a political force is an uncertain one. Many changes in technology are taking place which will change the ways in which television programmes and newspapers are produced. Who owns and who controls the media will still be important, whatever technology is being used to produce them.

very different and were introduced for different reasons and with different aims, but they would have provided more control over what we see. They were both unsuccessful. Arguments about the 'freedom of expression' were

Summary

Ownership and control over television broadcasting and newspaper publishing have been the focus for our understanding of the politics of the mass media. The degree to which individuals or groups can influence what they read or see on television is open to debate.

In 1986 Winston Churchill Junior, a Conservative MP, introduced a Bill into the House of Commons to limit scenes of sex and violence on television programmes including the news. At about the same time a Labour MP, Clare Short, introduced a Bill to prevent the 'Page 3 nudes' from appearing next to stories of rape and violence against women in the tabloid press. These Bills were

?

1 Read the editorial of the *Daily Express* and the *Daily Mirror* for the same day.
  - Identify what is bias, what is fact and what is opinion in them.
  - Analyse the editorials using the following checklist:

	Daily Express	Daily Mirror
Size of print		
Number of sentences		
Average length of sentences (i.e. number of words)		
Subject chosen		
Means of emphasizing main points (e.g. punctuation)		

  - Noting the differences you found, now write an editorial for each of these papers about an issue in which you are interested. Copy the style and bias used in each of the papers.

2 Watch the television news and make notes on:
  - the order of the news items
  - whether anyone is treated favourably
  - whether anyone is treated unfavourably

3 Using copies of several daily newspapers look at the pictures and consider the following questions:
  - What sorts of people are photographed for newspapers?
  - What sort of men appear in the newspapers and what are they doing?
  - What sort of women are photographed for newspapers and what are they doing?
  - Why do you think these images are chosen for newspapers?

7 · The politics of work

What is work and why do it?

There are many reasons why people work but there are three main ones:

- One of the most obvious reasons in an industrialized society like Britain is that work is a means of earning money. Money in itself is of no use to us. It is only useful because of the goods and services it can buy. There are three basic needs which all people need to satisfy. They are the needs for food, shelter and clothing or warmth. In our society we usually buy these things.

- Satisfaction from doing a job well, or because it helps oneself and others, is an important part of work. Satisfaction and enjoyment can come from the

Do you think people get satisfaction from working in these conditions?

work itself: doing something which requires care, skill and thought such as nursing. Satisfaction can come from being with other people and enjoying their company.

- Work also provides people with social status in our society. Surgeons have a high status job which brings with it influence and control over others and over their own lives.

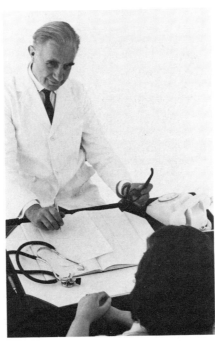

Why should the surgeon have higher status, better pay and more comfortable working conditions than the nurse?

Housework is low status and 'no-pay'. Why is this?

Such jobs, like those of a surgeon or a lawyer, have all of these rewards; high pay, a lot of satisfaction and high status. Some jobs have none.

For example, housework is unpaid, is rarely satisfying and has low status. Sometimes a person may say, 'I don't work, I'm just a housewife'. Nevertheless, housework is work and often hard work, and it is essential in providing for our basic needs. Food has to be bought and prepared, clothing has to be made, mended and washed, and shelter or housing has to be cleaned and maintained.

Money and conflict

At work some people earn more money than others. This unequal distribution of income is often accepted as normal or natural and it may not lead to conflict. Indeed some **pay negotiations** are based on the desire of some groups of workers to preserve **income differentials**, that is, to ensure that one group of workers continues to earn more than another group. Sometimes the differences between people's earnings are so great, or are considered to be so unfair, that conflicts do arise. Conflicts about pay and working conditions are often

	April 1979	April 1982	Percentage increase
	£	£	%
All non-manual males	113·00	178·90	58
All manual males	93·00	133·80	43·8
All males	101·40	154·40	52·3
Face-trained coal miners	126·70	180·90	42·7

Average gross weekly earnings, 1979–82

called industrial disputes. The dispute is usually between the management or the owners of a company and the workers.

How do conflicts arise?

In **capitalist** societies there is a potential conflict between the basic aims of workers and employers.

● Employers want to produce goods or services and sell them for as much money as they can. The cost of producing goods under capitalism includes: the equipment (management and buildings); the raw materials from which the goods are made; and the cost of wages for workers to operate the machinery, advertise, package and sell the goods. The employer needs to sell the goods for more money than it costs to make them. So the employer wants to keep the costs as low as possible, so that the profits made are as large as possible.

● The interests of the workers are often in conflict with the aims of the employer. Workers want to earn high wages and to work in pleasant conditions, where buildings and machinery are well-maintained and safe.

Supporters of capitalism argue that there is no conflict between employers and workers, because both have an interest in making profits. When profits are used to improve working conditions and to pay wages, both employers and workers benefit. However, profits come from selling goods and workers have to buy goods as well as make them. When the costs of goods go up workers need to earn more to pay for them. The employer might want to keep more of the profits made and so conflict arises.

In 1974 miners brought down a Conservative Government through their industrial action. Coal is a nationalized industry and the government is in some senses the employer

Who does the media usually blame for the effects of industrial disputes?

How are conflicts resolved?

Conflicts between workers and employers take many forms and are resolved in a variety of ways. Representatives of a work force, usually trade union leaders, meet managers, who represent the employers. They talk about the problems (such as low wages, unsafe machinery, unhealthy working conditions, hours of work, and holidays) and through discussions they try to reach an agreement. This process of negotiating and bargaining through discussion is a political activity.

Each group has interests, aims and some power.

- The management wants to keep production going, to keep costs down and to make a profit. Their power lies in their ownership and control over the capital (that is, machinery, property and buildings used to produce the goods) and in their capacity to offer income and the status of being employed to workers.
- The workers want to improve their conditions and to increase their earnings and to protect their jobs. Their power lies in their ability to stop working, to **withdraw labour**.

Usually industrial disputes are settled by compromises reached during talks and negotiations:

- employers offer a bit more than they originally did
- workers accept less than they originally asked for

Economic force

When agreement or compromise is not being reached, one side or the other might make threats to try to influence the outcome in their favour.

- The management could threaten redundancies or longer hours if workers do not accept low pay rises.
- The workers could threaten strike action if their pay claim is not met.
- Each side in the dispute presents facts and figures to support its argument and to try to convince the other side and the general public that it has a case.
- Management will often produce figures to show that the workers are asking for too much compared with other groups of workers, or that there is not enough money to meet their demands.
- Workers will often produce figures to show that their incomes have fallen in relation to other workers, or that the conditions they work in are dangerous.

In these ways the two sides in the dispute, through their representatives, achieve their aims by using political skills of argument,

reasoning, presenting information, appealing to others, manipulation and if all else fails economic force. Economic force can involve workers' withdrawing their labour or management making workers redundant. In this kind of dispute one side has more power to achieve its aims and to influence the outcome than the other.

Why is work important?

Work is an important area for political debate and action. Many people learn how to gain political power and how to use it through their experiences at work. But for large numbers of people this form of political action and power is not available: people who do not work in paid employment, such as:

- children
- retired people
- severely disabled people
- housewives
- the unemployed

They are often dependent on others such as parents or husbands or on State benefits like Social Security for their income. This puts them in a relatively powerless position. They are not well-organized into powerful political groups like the **CBI** or the **TUC**. Nevertheless some have formed **pressure groups** to try to gain power for themselves and others in similar positions.

Sometimes relatively powerless groups have to use their intelligence and imagination while others can rely on force

How does forming a group such as a Pensioners' Union help old people?

- Newspapers and magazines report what they say and do; even when this is not important, others follow or copy them.
- They have some power to influence the ideas of others through their access to the media.
- Their inherited title usually brings with it inherited wealth such as land or property, and this is an important political resource.

Status through employment

Some types of employment bring with them high status:

- They are usually white collar jobs, that is, professional and managerial
- They are non-manual jobs

Manual jobs are often given low status in our society, where there is a division between work which is considered to be intellectual and physical or manual work.

For example, sewing machinists earn only 76 per cent of the average full-time wage for a woman. This division is not based on how important or worthwhile the work is. Cleaners are very important for the health and welfare of all people at home, in shops, offices, factories or in the streets, but cleaning is low status work. Film producers have high status, but their work might not be useful or important.

For example
- Women have begun to establish loosely formed groups through the women's movement to talk about their political roles in the family, in relation to paid employment and in society in general.
- The Child Poverty Action Group was set up to protect the economic needs of children and to fight for better government **legislation** for children and families with children.
- Pensioners' groups and claimants' unions have been formed to protect the position of people on State benefits.

society. They have inherited high status. They may not have a lot of money, although most do, and they may not be very powerful, although **peers** do have the right to sit in the **House of Lords**. But what they do have is status, and this brings with it a certain amount of power:

Despite these pressure groups, many people without paid work (except for the very rich) remain isolated and powerless to change their own lives. Organizing with others improves their position, but they are still in relatively weak positions compared with those in paid employment.

Status

Inherited status

Members of the aristocracy, such as lords, ladies, dukes, earls etc, are in a particularly privileged section of

Do these old people need to form a union or a pressure group?

which require specialized treatment and can refer the patient to a hospital.

In Britain primary health care is the main responsibility of the general practitioner (GP), who has to train for at least seven years. GPs have a wide range of drugs at their disposal to prescribe for patients and they are usually well paid for their work either in the National Health Service or as private doctors. In cases of serious illness they can refer patients to hospitals.

Do these manual workers have high pay, status or job satisfaction?

So what or who makes the differences between high status and low status jobs? One reason for these differences is the power some groups have developed to define their own position in society as important.

An example – Doctors

China and Britain

In China **barefoot doctors** are used in local communities for primary medical care. They receive a very short training. They have a few medicines and with these they can treat most common ailments. They can diagnose more severe illnesses

Status

The social position of the GP in Britain is quite different from that of the barefoot doctors in China. Some reasons are :

- GPs have developed a situation where they can restrict entry to their profession by very rigid entry requirements to medical schools.
- They have removed medicine from general understanding by insisting upon long periods of training for 'experts'.
- They have secured high pay and status for themselves as a profession.

The power the GP has over people's lives, health and bodies is extensive. Many people in Britain have given up trying to understand or control their own health because the medical profession has successfully taken over that role for them:

- Traditional remedies, herbal cures and home-made medicine have given way to drugs produced from chemicals and prescribed by doctors.
- The patient often has no idea what these drugs contain or what the possible effects will be.
- The doctors themselves do not always understand how the drugs work or what bad effects, often called 'side-effects', they might have.
- People believe what their doctors tell them and take drugs without knowing why, except that the doctor prescribed them.

Alternatives

Some people have tried to regain control over their own health:

Hello Ms. Smith. I suffer from megalomania, how about you?

- Some women have set up Well-Woman Clinics. These clinics are intended to teach women how to look after themselves and how to treat themselves, so they can prevent most common ailments and deal with them themselves if they do become ill.

- Acupuncture, Homoeopathy and other types of medicine based on the treatment of the whole person (using natural remedies and the body's own defences) are becoming more popular in the West. In this small way people are trying to change their own position in relation to their health and the position which doctors have developed. They are questioning the social status and the power of doctors.

Doctors, solicitors and teachers have considerable power and control over the lives of others. Factory owners and other employers (who once controlled the lives of others at work) were among the first groups to have their power limited by government action.

The influence of the Government

The Factory Acts

The earliest activities of the British Government into the area of paid employment came in the 1830s, 1840s and 1870s with the Factory Acts. These Acts of Parliament put restrictions on the factory owners so that they could no longer legally **exploit** the workers, by making them work long hours in dangerous conditions. The Acts:

- limited the number of hours people could work at one time
- limited the age at which children could be employed
- limited the types of work and hours which women could do
- introduced regulations to fence off dangerous machinery and to prevent women and children from cleaning moving machines

The Ten Hour Limit

The political struggle in the nineteenth century to establish a ten

Why did employers use children and women to do these jobs before the Factory Acts were passed? Did the Acts stop all exploitation of workers?

hour work shift was a long and difficult one. Short-time committees made up of adult workers were set up to press the Government and factory owners to accept a ten hour shift for women and children. Some MPs from both the Whig (early Liberal) and the Tory (Conservative) parties supported the Ten Hour Movement, but many MPs and factory owners opposed it. The manufacturers feared that they would not be able to produce as much if laws limited the number of hours women and children could work. By the middle of the nineteenth century, after almost fifty years of struggle, the Ten Hour Limit for women and children was applied to some industries, mainly textiles, and production did not fall as some manufactueres had feared.

The motives behind MPs agreeing to reduce working hours for women were mixed:

- Some were concerned that the health and welfare of women and children were put at risk by working long hours.
- Others were worried that if women were in paid employment then they were not at home looking after the men, and so this Act could enable them to do two jobs, one at home and one in the factory.

It was not until the end of the nineteenth century that the working hours of men were limited by law.

Results of the Acts

However slow the Government was to take some responsibility for protecting workers, the Factory Acts *did* mark a change in the role of government in Britain. The Factory Acts established the principle that the Government had a right and a duty to intervene in the operation of the **free market** in order to protect the freedom of the majority against the exploitation of a minority.

This was an important stage, at a time when *laissez faire* (the freedom for the people to do as they liked or were able) was dominant in economic affairs. It had been thought unnecessary to pass laws which restricted employers in any way, because making a profit was important and how that profit was made was not. It was only later that the intervention of the government into the economic activities of manufacturers and other employers came to be seen as a way of protecting workers against unscrupulous employers, and not as an unnecessary restriction on personal freedom. However, the Factory Acts did not only operate to the advantage of the workers; employers also benefited by having a healthier workforce.

Since these early Factory Acts set the precedent, much more legislation has been introduced to improve conditions and opportunities at work.

The Sex Discrimination Act

In 1975 the Sex Discrimination Act and the Equal Pay Act came into effect. In employment the Sex Discrimination Act makes it illegal to discriminate on grounds of sex or marital status in training, promotion and recruitment. This means that men and women cannot be denied a job, training or promotion because of their sex or because they are married. The law applies to most areas of paid employment, but not all. Many women have been unable to take advantage of this legislation because of lack of child care facilities and the dominant attitude that women's role is to look after children.

The Equal Pay Act

The Equal Pay Act was not intended to make women's wages as high as men's, but to ensure that it would be illegal for an employer to pay different rates to men and women for doing the same or broadly similar work. Unfortunately, women and men very often do not do the same or broadly similar work.

> **For example,** only two per cent of the directors of British companies are women.

Men and women at work, 1970–84. Women's average hourly earnings as a percentage of men's

Women tend to be concentrated into a few types of employment such as the textile industries, clerical and catering work and the service industry, which have become defined as 'women's work'. In these sectors of employment men often do not work and so it is not possible to make comparisons between the work that women and men do, except in terms of work of equal value. The law in Britain does not yet include the idea that women and men should be paid the same for work of equal value. At present, the average woman's wage is less than three quarters that of the average man, despite the Equal Pay Act.

Trade unions

In 1799 the Combination Act was passed to make all trade unions, or combined groups of workers, illegal. This was done because:

- Employers feared the power of people when they were able to press for better pay and working

In 1834 these farm labourers (later known as the Tolpuddle Martyrs) were deported for trying to set up a trade union. About the same time working-class men were executed for damaging new machinery which took away their jobs

conditions by taking collective action.
- Many landowners feared that an uprising like the French Revolution could happen in Britain also, if working people had too much power.

Despite the Combination Act working people in industries such as mining and textiles continued to meet and to discuss their working conditions. By doing so they put themselves in danger of being prosecuted under the law for attempting to increase wages or decrease working hours, or for persuading other workers to combine together to do the same. It was mainly because workers refused to comply with the law and continued to organize themselves, preferring to be prosecuted, that the Combination Act was repealed in 1824. After that trade unions became legal, albeit with many restrictions on their organization and activities.

Trade unions have increased in power in particular industries, but Industrial Relations Acts passed in the 1970s and 80s have tried to limit the power of trade unions by controlling their activities in relation to **industrial action**, picketing, and their organization in places of work.

How much control over her work does this cashier have? Can she make decisions about what she does or how?

bottom. If everyone accepts their position in the hierarchy, then the business can get on and produce goods or services without disruption.
- A different argument is that industry would be better run if workers could take part in some management decisions. This could be arranged by workers electing representatives to sit on the board of managers.
- A third view is that the distinction between management and workers need not exist at all and that it is possible to create work situations where everybody has some power over what they do and how they do it, both individually and collectively.

Alternatives and change

Most people have very little control over the type of work they do or how they do it. For the majority of workers, what they do and how they do it is determined by others.

For example
- Nurses are not in a powerful position to change the way a hospital is organized
- Shop assistants cannot decide what they sell
- Factory workers do not usually make decisions about what the factory will produce

- Some people argue that this is how it ought to be. The **hierarchy** in most work places means that the people at the top make decisions for workers at the

Ways to organize the workplace

The Lucas Plan: a case study

In the early 1970s the workers at several Lucas Aerospace factories, which made parts for armaments, were threatened with redundancies by the management. In response to the threats of unemployment and a growing concern about the dangers of war to which their products contributed, a number of shop stewards got together to draw up a plan which became known as the Lucas Plan.

The aim of the Plan

The object of the Lucas Plan was:

> 'to fight for secure, useful and dignified jobs for those whose skills and energies are at present wasted; to provide training, especially to women and youths, and to make products which would help not worsen human problems'.

Three main areas

Their Plan considered three main areas:

The problems of unemployment

They saw fewer people being needed in all forms of work because of the recession, cuts in government spending, and the use of new technology which meant money was spent on machines and not on workers' wages.

Their aim was not to *reject* the new technology, but to *control* it and to devise a plan which would create more jobs not fewer.

Boring work

They saw that over the last seventy years many jobs in industry had become boring and repetitive, requiring less and less skill and training. Jobs had become more and more divided up into small and narrow functions, a process known as the division of labour, so that workers could not see the point of what they were doing and had become deskilled. Their aim was to create jobs which used the skills and intelligence which they believed all workers possessed and could develop.

The fear of war and the danger of arms production

They were concerned that the machinery and technology owned by Lucas Aerospace was being used to help to produce weapons of destruction. Their aim was to produce a plan which would show how the existing plant, the machinery, technology and other equipment, could be used to produce socially useful goods.

Socially-useful production

The shop stewards involved in this did a lot of research over six years and eventually produced a plan which included all of their aims. Central to the plan was the idea of socially-useful production. This included not only the goods to be produced but also the ways in which they would be produced:

- the process
- the product

The process

The process they suggested in the plan involved:

- a breakdown in the differences between management, scientific staff and workers
- people's jobs were to be put before profits
- the right of the management to manage without being accountable to the workers was challenged
- the authority of management was questioned and replaced by popular control over all social, economic and political decisions

The Lucas Plan presented ways in which representative democracy, whereby workers voted for union leaders or elected worker managers, could be replaced by a system in which all workers might be involved in decision-making.

The product

The sort of socially-useful products they envisaged and researched for the plan included medical equipment (such as aids for the disabled and kidney machines); alternative ways of producing energy for heating and lighting (such as solar cells, heat pumps and windmills); new transport systems which would be less polluting than cars and would use up less energy; new vehicles in which people could work safely under water; and remote control equipment so that dangerous jobs could be performed by robots, controlled in safety from a distance.

Results of the Plan

These plans required a change in the politics of work, and a commitment to worker self-management and social ownership of the means of production, that is, the **capital equipment**, buildings, machinery etc.

However, the Plan was rejected by the Lucas Aerospace Company;

- The Labour Government supported the company
- The Plan did receive support from workers at Lucas
- Over a thousand workers at Lucas Aerospace were made redundant
- Lucas continue to make armaments

Summary

The politics of work is mainly concerned with settling disputes peacefully. Money, status and power are important features of work which influence decision-making and the control which people have over their activities at work. Although the Lucas Plan did not succeed there has been an increase in the number of small businesses run on cooperative lines. Cooperatives, where profits are shared and decisions are made collectively, are an attempt to practice democracy in the workplace.

1. Interview parents, guardians and other adults about what they did when they left school. Ask them why they left and what choices they had.
   - Ask them how important money, status and job satisfaction is to them.

2. Use recent newspapers to find out about an industrial dispute which is happening at the moment. Try to find out how the dispute started and what the different arguments are.
   In a group take the various roles in the dispute, so that some of you are representatives of management and others are representing the workers. Try to reach an agreement through negotiations.

3. Use copies of the magazines *Tatler* and *Country Life*. Try to construct a day in the life of a member of the aristocracy. You can pretend to be them if you want to.
   - Describe your day as carefully as you can using the ideas from the magazines to help you.
   - Re-read your description of your day and try to pick out all the times when you were in control of your own life, doing what you wanted, and the times when you were in control of the lives of others.

4. What do you think is meant by 'work of equal value'? If you were writing an amendment to the Equal Pay Act (see page 57) to include the idea that women and men who do work of equal value should be paid the same, how would you express this? Give examples to show what you mean by 'work of equal value'.
   - Do you think that such a change in the law would make any differences? Would men be more likely to apply for jobs in areas which have been traditionally 'women's work'?
   - Might women be forced out of work as a result of such a change? What would encourage women to apply for jobs in areas which have traditionally been 'men's work'?

5. Take your school as an example of a place where people go to work. Draw a diagram to show hierarchy (the order of positions) of the staff who work there. Start with the person in the top position (the Headteacher, school keeper or whoever you think has the most power in the school) and work down to staff in lower positions. You could use a triangle shape for example. Include all the staff (teachers, school keepers, office and kitchen staff for example) and indicate on your diagram which staff are male and which are female. What does this show you?

6. Conduct a survey. Write to employers in your area (include the local council, the Area Health Authority and Local Education Authority as well as private businesses). You will find their addresses in your local *phone book*. Ask them the following questions:
   - Do they have an Equal Opportunities Policy?
   - Do they know how many of their employees are from ethnic minorities?
   - Do they think this is important or not?
   - Do they actively try to recruit women or black applicants to jobs they advertise?

Record your findings. What do they show you?

8 · The politics of democracy

What is democracy?

Democracy is generally thought to be a good means of government. Schools, clubs and trade unions often pride themselves on being democratic, as do national governments. Several different types of governments and nations describe themselves as being democratic. Countries as different as the USSR, India, Britain, the USA and China all claim to be democracies.

We are going to consider:

- the various meanings of democracy
- the different ways in which it is practised

The People's Congress in Xiamen, south east China

Classical democracy

The word democracy comes from two Greek words which when translated mean *people power*.

Origins

The origins of our ideas about democracy come from the ancient Greek city-state of Athens. In Athens they practised a form of direct democracy in which all qualified citizens were expected to take part in the government of the city. Outdoor public meetings were held as often as forty times a year to decide everything from how public money should be spent, to whether or not to go to war. Everyone there had a right to speak and decisions were taken by a majority vote of all those present.

Congress in the USA. Why do both China and the USA both describe themselves as democracies?

This system is often held up as the ideal form of participative direct democracy. However, even in Athens not all people were considered to be qualified citizens. Women, slaves and anyone under eighteen years old were excluded from the democratic processes.

Nevertheless, Athens was far more democratic than other states of the time. Most countries were ruled by a monarch or another unelected leader (such as an emperor or tyrant) or by an oligarchy (a group of a few nobles). So most people were not part of the government at all.

- It was thought by the nobility that the mass of the people were not capable of governing themselves or of taking any part in government.
- The nobles believed that only they had the necessary education, background and inherited qualities to make good decisions.

The idea that democracy is not possible without high levels of education and that some people are born to be leaders still persists today. However, there are more and more examples from industry in this country and in Third World countries to show that all sorts of people, even those without formal education and qualifications, can make sensible decisions about their own lives.

Development

Towards the end of the eighteenth century democracy began to re-emerge in Europe. The all-powerful rule of monarchs was threatened by the French Revolution, and to prevent it spreading to other countries more people were allowed to vote. By then the nations in which democracy was developing were much larger than Athens. This led to the development of representative democracy. Instead of all qualifying citizens being involved in their own government, systems of **indirect democracy** developed in which the people (adult men at first and only later women) **elected** their **representatives**. These representatives made decisions on behalf of the people who elected them.

A Chartist procession, 1848. Chartism was a national working-class movement which campaigned for the vote for all men

During the nineteenth century two different views of democracy emerged and both of them exist today:

- democracy as an ideal
- democracy as a system

An ideal or a system?

Democracy as an ideal

- The people who supported this view were mainly those who were fighting for a working class party.
- They saw democracy as a way to give more people the opportunity to take part in government.
- They wanted power and control to be shared more equally so that all people could be involved in determining their own lives.

From this view democracy is an ideal to be worked towards. The political system would need to change to include more people in more ways of making decisions. Democracy as an ideal, was becoming popular at the beginning of this century.

Democracy as a system

- This view of democracy was supported by those already in power in the Government; Liberals and Conservatives.

- They saw democracy as a way of choosing a government.
- Democracy for them meant giving people the vote so they could elect leaders. Once the vote had been extended to include all adults, then democracy had been achieved.

In this sense of democracy people do not have any direct part in government, only an indirect one through their elected representatives. The influence of this second version of democracy as a system has been the strongest of the two in Britain.

Elitism

Elite theories

To counter this growing popularity, and in particular the ideas of Marx, a group of writers developed an **elite theory** of democracy. According to this theory democracy is not possible because there will always be a few people at the top of society, an elite, who are better suited to govern than others. Elections can be a democratic way of choosing between these elite groups, but the majority of people are not suited to leadership, or indeed self-government.

Democratic elitism

From this point of view power will always be in the hands of the few, but the majority have the right to choose between competing elites. Whichever group is chosen must govern for the benefit of the majority, or else they will be thrown out by the voters at the next election.

This theory fits in with the view of democracy as a system in which voting is the major political activity for most of the people. Other forms of direct participation in government are seen to be unnecessary or undesirable.

The theory of democratic elitism justifies describing Britain as a democracy, but not Communist countries such as the USSR because they do not have elite groups or political parties competing for the people's votes. They only have one elite group, the Communist party; no organized opposition is allowed, and so are described as **totalitarian** systems. However, the USSR itself claims to be a people's democracy, and indeed to be more democratic than most western countries such as the USA, Britain and other European countries.

People's democracy

Countries such as China and the USSR, are often described as Communist countries. These are examples of how people's democracies, or **proletarian** democracies, can justify the description 'democratic'.

China and the USSR became people's democracies after **revolutions** during which the old systems of government were completely overturned and replaced by new governments which claimed to represent the majority of the people.

The Communist party

The Communist party is said to be the way in which the majority are represented. It expresses the wishes of the majority of the people and acts in their interests. The Communist party forms the government and so the claims for a democratic government arise from the position

Young Pioneers in Cuba learn the ideals of Communism

This family felt they could not practise their religion freely in the USSR

of the party as the organ of the people.

Criticism suppressed

Since the party is said to represent 'the people', anyone who criticizes it or attacks it is said to be attacking 'the people'. This reasoning allows governments like the USSR to supress criticism. Recently, it has been argued in the USSR that communism is the best form of government and all reasonable people would accept this. Anyone who does not accept it and opposes the Soviet system must be

unreasonable and mentally unbalanced. This argument has been used in the USSR to justify the sending of some **dissidents** to mental hospitals. This has led to criticism from western democracies and strengthened their claim that the USSR is not a democracy because it does not allow freedom of speech and opposition. However, officials in the USSR argue that freedom of speech is allowed as long as it does not put in danger the Communist party and therefore the wishes of the people.

The degree to which criticism and opposition are allowed varies from one communist country to another. It is not a necessary part of a people's democracy to ban criticism, but it has become so in the USSR. This has come to be seen by some within and many outside the Soviet Union as an intolerable lack of personal freedom. It is justified by the Soviet Communist party as necessary in the short term, to enable real democracy in the long term. In the true communist society to which they aim, such restrictions and interference will not be necessary and will not exist, because the party will genuinely represent the people.

Liberal democracy

Liberal democracy is a term used to describe the kind of representative democracy which exists in Britain, most of western Europe and the USA. Pressure groups and Political parties are essential to the idea and the work of liberal democracies.

Pressure groups

Pressure groups exist to represent and defend a variety of interests within a liberal democracy. They are sometimes called 'interest groups',

Whose interests are being promoted here?

because their aim is to defend or to promote the interests of their members and supporters.

> Pressure groups do not try to gain the sort of political power necesary to form a government, but seek to influence political parties and decision makers who will then act on their behalf.

There are two main types of pressure groups:

- promotional groups
- protective groups

Promotional groups

These pressure groups promote a particular cause.

> **For example,** the Campaign for Nuclear Disarmament (CND) is one such group. Its aim is to promote the cause of nuclear disarmament. It tries to influence government decisions in a variety of ways, including demonstrations, marches, petitions, advertising and public meetings.

Protective groups

These pressure groups aim to protect their members and the interests of their members.

> **For example,** trade unions, professional associations and the CBI are groups which try to protect their members by influencing government decisions:
> - the CBI represents the interests of the owners of businesses
> - the trade unions represent the interests of employees

There is often overlap between these two types of pressure groups. They both use similar methods:

- trying to gain public support for their causes
- taking action (such as the methods used by **CND**)
- providing the Government and especially the Civil Service with important and specialized information
- contributing money to the funds of a political party. In Britain the trade unions contribute money to the Labour party, while businesses donate money to the Conservative party

Arguments for and against

Those who support liberal democracy as an ideal argue that pressure groups are an important way in which people can influence governments in addition to voting at elections. They claim that pressure groups ensure that power is spread among a wide range of groups so that all major interests in society have some power and some control over the actions of governments.

Critics of liberal democracy argue that the poorest, weakest, and most powerless groups in society are not

Whose interests are being protected here?

able to organize themselves effectively into a pressure group and so influence the Government. Some causes are considered seriously by government, but others are not considered to be important issues.

Political parties

> Political parties, unlike pressure groups, try to gain power and exercise it themselves by forming a government.

They appeal to a wider range of interests than pressure groups. Nevertheless, they tend to attract support from one section of the population more than another.

Support
- In Britain, the Labour party gains support mainly from the working class and trade union movement, but also from parts of the middle class, especially from new professions in public services like teachers and social workers.

- The Conservative party has traditionally won support from the middle class, and about four fifths of the middle class vote Conservative. However, about a third of the working class also vote for the Conservative party, and this is a significant proportion.

- The Liberal/Social Democratic Party Alliance is trying to gain support from the middle ground of middle class and working class voters who are disillusioned with the other two parties and believe that a compromise between the positions of the two other parties is possible.

Elections
Elections to form a government from the political parties are an important part of liberal democracies. The elections are secret so that no one is pressurized or forced to vote in a particular way, and all voters cast their votes in a secret ballot. The votes are counted in various ways.

In many European countries a system of proportional representation is used. There are two main forms of proportional representation:

- the *list system*, used in most European countries, in which each party presents a list of candidates and wins the number of seats in a **constituency** according to the number of votes cast for the party list
- the *single transferable vote* which enables voters to mark all

candidates for whichever party in order of preference. When the votes are counted the candidates with the least number of votes are eliminated and their votes are redistributed according to the voters' order of preference

In both of these systems each political party can have more than one candidate standing in each constituency. This is known as multi-member constituencies. These methods ensure that seats in the government are allocated in proportion to the number of votes cast.

In Britain the method of voting and allocating seats in Parliament is called 'a simple majority' or 'first past the post'. Each constituency has only one candidate from each political party and each voter has only one vote – single member constituency and single vote. The party which elects the most MPs forms the Government, but because each MP is elected by a majority in a constituency, it is possible that there might be more votes cast over the whole country for a party which does not win the most seats (i.e., MPs in Parliament).

"If they're going to have another election they're not coming round the second time kissing and patting us on our heads."

Daily Express, March 5th, 1974

What methods do political parties use to win votes?

For example, a party that came a close second in a large number of constituencies, and so had received many people's votes, could still have no MPs.

This system is not necessarily fair, but it leads to stronger governments which do not have to compromise. There is a lot of debate about which system is fairest and which best reflects public opinion.

Each of the main political parties is seen as having different aims and policies, but all operate within the liberal democratic tradition, which means that they have to attract and keep the support of the electorate. In this way strong and stable government is ensured, but it also means that dramatic changes are unlikely to take place as this could lose public support.

Liberal democracy in Britain

In Britain there are certain principles on which democracy is founded. These are, on the whole, unwritten principles, unlike those of the American Constitution.

Freedom of speech

In theory

Freedom of speech means that, in theory, any view, however extreme, can be expressed. Criticisms can be made of government decisions. Criticisms of the very system of government can be spoken or written. This is an important aspect of British society, which offers the power of the freedom of speech to all citizens.

In practice

In practice there are limits to the extent of free speech:

- The laws of libel and slander limit what can be written or spoken about another person. This is to protect individuals whose lives and characters could be damaged if freedom of speech meant that

Speakers' corner in Hyde Park is a symbol of free speech

anyone could say or write anything, however untrue or unfounded it might be.

- The Government can issue D-notices forbidding journalists to print certain pieces of security information. This means that information which the Government believes the public

should not know can be kept secret.

- The freedom to speak publicly through the use of television or newspapers may be limited simply because it is difficult to get at these important forms of communication. This means that well-known people are able to express their views in public, but ordinary people find it difficult to appear on television or to have articles published in newspapers.

Freedom of association

Meetings

This means that anyone can call a public meeting, a rally or a demonstration and any number of people can attend. This is an important aspect of democratic political organization: members of pressure groups need to be able to meet to show the extent of their support in order to influence members of the public and the Government. However, there have been occasions when the Home Secretary has banned marches or demonstrations because it was felt that they would be likely to cause a major disturbance.

For example, the National Front was effectively banned from holding a rally by this action, but so were antifascist groups demonstrating against the National Front.

Police and pickets outside a Scottish mine during the miner's strike in 1984. Police are defending the right to work and pickets are upholding the right to withdraw labour. Why did these rights conflict?

Picketing

Picketing

Picketing is a form of association which has been restricted by the law. Limits imposed on the freedom of association and on the freedom of speech are justified as being necessary to protect the freedom and the peace of others.

Freedom from arbitrary arrest and equality in law

Arbitrary arrest means unjustified or random arrest. A person can only be arrested if he or she is charged with committing an offence in law. The freedom from arbitrary arrest does not apply to suspected terrorists or bombers, under the Prevention of Terrorism Act.

Equality before the law is important if all people are to be protected by the law. Laws are not intended to apply to some people or sections of society and not to others. Wealth or social status ought not to exempt anyone from the law. However, the ways in which the laws are applied depends to some extent on the judgement of the police.

> **For example,** some black community groups have argued that black youths are more likely to be stopped and searched than white youths.

How votes were cast for the three main political parties in the 1983 general election by social class differences (percentages)

Labour Party poster – would this poster win your vote?

It has been said that in the courts, 'the law is open to all, like the Ritz Hotel', meaning that some people can afford to pay expensive fees for solicitors and barristers to defend them. It is possible that this might influence the decisions of juries, when they are hearing cases.

Universal suffrage and elections every five years

Who can vote?

Universal suffrage means that all adults, that is, everyone over the age of eighteen, can vote if they are on the current register of electors and are British subjects or citizens of the Republic of Ireland.

People disqualified from voting are:

- aliens
- prisoners serving a sentence of more than one year
- people who have been found guilty of corrupt practices at elections

Peers can vote in local elections but not in general elections. The range of people who are allowed to vote has been extended by stages. At first only wealthy men could vote, then all men over twenty-one, then some women, and now all men and women over eighteen years old except those legally disqualified.

Does every vote count?

Even though virtually everyone over eighteen has a vote, not all votes are equally important at a general election.

- If you live in a constituency which is considered to be a safe seat, (that is, one in which one party has a massive majority) then votes for another party are not very important.
- In marginal seats, where support is more evenly distributed between two or more parties, then each vote matters more to the eventual outcome.

Voting every five years

Elections held at least every five years mean that the party chosen at the last election cannot afford to sit back when in government, or to pass a series of unpopular policies. They have to go back to the voters in five years to be rejected or chosen again.

However, people do not only vote on the basis of a party's record while in government, or on their proposed policies. People cast their vote for a particular political party:

- on the basis of how their parents voted
- along class lines
- for the overall image of a party, rather than for particular policies. A party which is able, through its use of the media, to project a popular image may win more

SDP poster – an attempt to win votes from the two main political parties

The higher education of MPs from all political parties in 1983

votes than other parties with equally sound policies

The system of voting

It is possible that none of the political parties or candidates at an election will reflect the whole range and diversity of opinion among the electorate. So people are forced to vote for a candidate who only represents part of what they want.

> **For example,** most governments since the Second World War have not had the support of the majority of the electorate.

Our system of voting enables a party which has less than half the votes cast across the country to take a large proportion of the seats in the House of Commons and so form the Government.

It is very difficult to win a seat at a general election as an independent candidate, who is not a member of one of the major political parties. Even the smaller political parties, such as the liberals, find difficulty in gaining a seat under our system of elections.

The MPs

The leaders of the political parties and indeed many of the MPs are mainly from social and economic backgrounds unlike the majority of the population:

- a high proportion of both Labour and Conservative MPs are from middle class, professional backgrounds
- many were educated at public schools
- few are women or black

The people have very little control over who their leaders are, only some control over which general policies their parties will pursue.

Open Government

Anyone can go to the House of Commons and sit in the public gallery to hear debates and decisions being made. Parts of the debates from the House of Commons are broadcast on the radio, but they are not televised. However, there are decisions made that are not made openly and that, as all political parties have argued, are necessarily secret.

The Government has the power to make secret decisions concerning issues to do with defence and security. Facts and decisions which it believes the public, but especially foreign governments, should not know about, can be kept secret.

The 1911 Official Secrets Act allows British governments to keep information about individual people without allowing them to know this information is kept about them.

> **For example,** this might include details about their private lives, their political activities, who they associate with and how much money they have.

This lack of openness in government is seen by some people to be an unacceptable use of government privilege and power.

The separation of powers

This separation of powers into areas is intended to stop power being concentrated in the hands of a few and to spread the exercise of power more widely.

The Legislature

> This is the role of Parliament – law-making or **legislation**.

Conservative Party poster – who were they trying to win votes from?

How Government works

Parliament includes:

- the House of Commons, where the elected representatives (M.P.s) formulate, debate and pass laws.
- the House of Lords, which is made up of **life peers** and **hereditary peers**. They debate the bills passed on to them by the House of Commons, but they can only delay the passage of a bill, they cannot reject it entirely.

The Queen is head of Parliament and she eventually signs the bills passed to her, to make them into Acts of Law.

The Executive

> This is the role of the Civil Service and government – putting laws into practice.

Civil Servants are paid employees of central government. It is the job of Civil Servants to provide politicians with information and to draw up policy proposals.

The Judiciary

> This is the role of the courts and judges – deciding whether laws have been broken and if so what punishment, treatment or compensation is suitable.

Arguments for and against

While these aspects of government are to some extent separate, there is also considerable overlap between them.

In so far as they are separate, they do act as forms of checks and balances against the excesses of each aspect of government. The powers to make laws, to put them into practice and to enforce them are spread between more people than if all these functions were in the hands of the same people, as in the case of a **military government**.

However, it can be argued that the people in positions of power in all three areas of government are from very similar social class and educational backgrounds and so form a ruling elite. According to this view, power is spread between members of this group, but not more widely among the population in general.

Summary

- **The way you see power distributed within a democracy will depend on your view of the world.**
- **Whether you see some countries as democracies and others as not will depend on your definition of democracy.**

We have mentioned two main ways of seeing the world and the society we live in, the consensus and conflict views.

A consensus view

- **A consensus view of society would suggest that Britain is a democracy but that the USSR is a totalitarian regime.**
- **From this view, power in Britain would be seen as being shared between various groups who all compete for influence and power.**

A conflict view

- **A conflict view of society would suggest that very few societies are real democracies, because democracy is still an ideal way of decision-making to work towards.**
- **From this view, power in Britain would be seen as being concentrated in the hands of a few ruling groups, while the majority of people remain relatively powerless for most of the time.**

1 What is meant by *democracy*? Give examples of democratic processes at home, at school or in other areas of life in which you have been involved.

2 What reasons can you give for excluding some people from decision-making? Why were women, slaves and children not allowed to take part in the democracy in Athens?

3 What are the differences between democracy as an *ideal* and democracy as a *system*?

4 What is an *elite?*

5 Can you think of any examples of situations where allowing people to write or say anything they liked could be a danger?

6 What arguments would you use, if you were the Home Secretary, to justify banning a National Front demonstration?

7 Why do you think that so few women and black men go into politics? Does it matter if they do or not?

8 What sort of information might a government want to keep about individuals? How could this be a danger to personal freedom?

9 What is the value of having a House of Lords? Could the members of the 'second chamber' be chosen in another way?

Extension activities

Chapter 1 · Politics

Conduct two surveys to show how much power different groups of people have to make their own decisions.

1 Conduct a short survey of people your own age to find out what things they can decide for themselves. For example you might ask them whether they can decide:

- where they go in the evening
- who their friends are
- what to wear
- where to go on holiday
- what to do when they leave school
- what to watch on TV
- what to eat

You could make a list of questions and ask them to tick a box 'Yes' or 'No'.

2 Do the same survey but with older people.

3 Compare the results of the two surveys. What do they show you?

4 You could also do the same surveys but between people from different ethnic backgrounds, or between male and female for example.

Chapter 2 · The politics of schooling

1 Take photographs of areas around your school which teachers rarely see (the toilets, graffiti, behind the gym for example). Compare these photos with those of the school in the school prospectus or magazine. What are the differences? Who decides what will be the public view of the school?

2 Organize a visit to a school which is very different from your own (fee-paying or state, mixed or single-sex for example).

To do this you will need to write to the Headteacher of the school you want to visit. You can find the address of the school and the name of its Headteacher in 'The Education Year Book' (published by the Longman Group Ltd, Longman House, Burnt Mill, Harlow, Essex CM20 2JE). Your school will have a copy. Or, if it is a local school, you could use the telephone directory.

In your letter to the Headteacher:

- explain who you are
- explain why you want to visit the school
- suggest some dates when you could go

It would also be helpful to include:

- a copy of the questions you want to ask
- a list of the people you want to talk to (e.g. the Headteacher; the School Keeper; a young classroom teacher; some pupils from the 1st, 2nd, 3rd, 4th, 5th years etc.).

Before you write up your list of questions, decide what it is you want to find out and work out questions which will extract the information you want. For instance you might ask:

- What is your position in the school?
- Do you have school rules?
- Who decided what the rules would be?
- What kinds of punishments and rewards are there?

You could then ask the same questions of similar people in your own school. How does this school compare with your own?

Chapter 3 · The politics of gender

Try to arrange to see one or more of the following 'feminist' films/videos:

- Rosie the Rivetter
- Take it like a Man, Ma'am
- The Color Purple
- A Question of Silence

You can contact video shops (addresses in the telephone directory) to see if they are available on video, or write to Concorde Films (Concorde Films Council Ltd, 201 Felixstowe Road, Ipswich, London; tel 760 12).

Chapter 4 · The politics of the family

Using pictures from magazines or your own drawings, make a mock-up for an advertisement for breakfast cereal showing an alternative family or household to the type usually shown in advertisements (see photograph on page 24 for example). Do you think this would achieve the aim of selling the product?

Chapter 5 · The politics of racism

Invite people to speak to your class on the politics of racism locally. You might invite someone from the Council for Racial Equality, someone from a local ethnic community group, and someone from a local newspaper or radio programme.

- You can write to The Commission for Racial Equality (Elliot House, Allington Street, London SW) for addresses of local organizations
- Your Local Council at the Town Hall (address from the telephone directory) might also have names and addresses of local ethnic community groups.
- You could also write to Channel 4 Television (Channel 4 Television Company, 60 Charlotte Street, London W1; tel 01–0631 4444) to see if someone from their

Multi-Cultural Programme department could come to speak to your class.

Chapter 6 · The politics of the mass media

Imagine that the BBC has decided not to broadcast a documentary film about South Africa, because the controller of programmes says it is biased.

In your class decide who will be:

- the film maker
- the controller of programmes
- some people in the film who want it to be shown
- the BBC Board of Governors who are divided in their opinions

Act out the discussion which might take place to decide whether or not the film will in fact be shown.

Chapter 7 · The politics of work

Arrange a visit to a YTS training scheme. You can write to the Manpower Services Commission (use the telephone directory to find tho addrocc of your *looal* offiooo) for schemes near you. You can also find information about these from your local Job Centre or Careers Office (see telephone directory for addresses).

Interview a trainee, a trainer and the manager or employer. Try to find out if there are any differences in the views of people involved in the scheme over things like conditions of work, value of the training, prospects, rates of pay, status, trade union activity etc.

Chapter 8 · The politics of democracy

Organize a mock election with members of political parties (real or imaginary) putting forward their case for why they should be elected to form a government. Write to the Town Hall to find the addresses of your local party headquarters (use the telephone directory). Write to the agents for the political parties and ask them if they can send a representative to a debate with members of other political parties.

Glossary

The words in the Glossary appear in bold in the text when first used.

Act of Parliament: law passed by **Parliament**

anarchy: state of complete freedom from rules and constraints

authority: generally accepted right to exercise **power**

autocratic: system in which there is one person or a small group making decisions and having the **power** to enforce them

autonomy: freedom to determine one's own actions or to act independently

barefoot doctors: local people trained for six months in basic medical knowledge, working in Chinese villages as part of a team of community health workers

cabinet: inner circle of ministers controlling government policy

capital equipment: factories, machinery etc. which is used to provide goods and services

capitalist state: system in which land, buildings, factories and equipment for producing goods are privately owned

CBI: Confederation of British Industry: a group of owners, managers and directors who represent the interests of employers

CND: Campaign for Nuclear Disarmament

constituency: electoral area within which voters choose their **representatives**

constitution: underlying principles which guide the laws of a society or other group

consultative democracy: system in which people's views and opinions are sought but decisions are made by a minority

cultures: peoples' entire ways of life, including their values, attitudes and beliefs

democratic: system in which people share power and participate in making decisions

DES: Department of Education and Science

despot: all-powerful ruler

dissidents: people who disagree with and speak out against their society (usually associated with a **totalitarian** state)

elected representative: voted for or chosen through the ballot bax or by a show of hands

elite theory: idea that a small number of people are best suited to govern over the majority

EOC: Equal Opportunities Commission

ethnicity: people's cultural and national background, relating to race

exploitation: process whereby a powerful person or group of people are able to use others for their own purposes

extended family: large family unit which includes *more* than two generations living together or near each other and having regular contact

free market: absence of government controls over the economy (e.g. no wage or price controls and no limits on trading)

GLC: Greater London Council

hereditary peers: people who are born with a title which they inherited from their parents and pass on to their children

hierarchy: system in which people have set places in a graded order. Often a small group at the top have power over the majority of people below them

House of Commons: lower house in the British system of government, composed of elected **representatives**

House of Lords: upper house, or second chamber, in the British process of government, composed of **peers**

IBA: Independent Broadcasting Association

ILEA: Inner London Education Authority

income differentials: differences in levels of pay between groups or workers in the same industry

indirect democracy: see **representative democracy**

industrial action: to **strike**, work-to-rule or go-slow as part of **industrial disputes**

industrial disputes: arguments between managers and workers, often involving **industrial action** taken to try to resolve the disagreement

legislation: the making of laws

life peers: people who are given a title which they have for the rest of their lives but which they cannot pass on to their children

manipulate: to produce a result by the ability to control and influence a situation, often in hidden ways

military government: state in which officers of the army, the navy or the airforce run a country, usually by force

nuclear family: basic family unit including two generations, usually parent(s) and children living together and having close contact

Parliament: supreme law-making body in Britain, consisting of the **House of Commons** and the **House of Lords**

participative direct democracy: system in which everyone is involved in sharing power and making decisions themselves, rather than through **representatives**

party politics: discussion and competition between organized political groups which form the government and the opposition

patrials: people who have the right to live in a country because their parents or grandparents were born there

patriarchy: system in which men have **power** over women

pay negotiations: discussion between **representatives** of workers and management over wages

peers: nobles who may sit in the **House of Lords**

power: ability to achieve one's aims, to exert influence over others, overcoming resistance

private member's bill: bill put to **Parliament** by an ordinary M P of any political party who is not a Cabinet member

pressure groups: self-organized groups of people who try to influence government decisions and public opinion

proletarian: relating to wage-earners without property, land or means of earning a living except by working for others. (This group can also include the unemployed and wageless who must depend on State benefits.)

representative democracy: system of sharing **power** and making decisions in which the majority elect a few people to act on their behalf (also called **indirect democracy**)

representatives: few people who act on behalf of a larger number of people

revolution: a complete change in a political system

sexism: prejudice and discrimination against people, usually women, because of their sex

state: organized political community under one government

status: person's position in society in relation to other individuals and groups; the respect and prestige given to people because of their positions in society

status quo: things as they are, without changes

stereotypes: standardized images of individuals or groups of people which are based on wrong or exaggerated information

strike: to **withdraw labour**, to stop working as part of **industrial action**

subordinate: being in second place or inferior to others

totalitarian: relating to a form of government where the State has no formal opposition; a one-party system

tripartite system of education: set up by the 1944 Education Act to provide three types of secondary school: grammar, technical and secondary modern

TUC: Trades Union Congress: an association of different trade unions which represent the interests of employees

withdraw labour: to stop working or go on **strike**

Index

Act of Parliament 3, 22, 71
Advertisements 16, 17, 24, 45, 48
Anarchy 26, 71
Attitudes 5, 12, 33, 35, 44
Authority 4, 7, 71
Autocratic 9, 71
Autonomy 9, 71

Barefoot doctors 55, 71
Beliefs 5, 12, 33
Bias 43, 48
Butler Education Act 12
Butler, Joyce 22

Cabinet 30, 71
Campaign for Nuclear Disarmament
  (CND) 49, 64, 71
Capital equipment 60, 71
Capitalism 52, 71
Church of England 7
Church shools 11
Charity schools 11
Civil Service 69
Commonwealth Immigration Act (1962)
  38
Communist party 48, 63–64
Comprehensive schools 13
Confederation of British Industries (CBI)
  53, 64, 71
Constituency 65, 67, 71
Constitution 66, 71
Conflict 3, 4, 5, 19, 20, 26, 43, 52, 53, 69
Consciousness raising 23
Consultative democracy 25, 71
Classical democracy 61–62
Consensus 4, 42, 69
Conservative party 7, 11, 23, 42, 47, 64
Control 9, 19, 20, 21, 42, 43, 51, 56, 59
Coote, Anna 23
Councillor 10, 13
Council for Racial Equality (CRE) 36
Culture 33, 71

Decision-making 3, 25, 49, 60, 69
Democracy 61–69
Democratic 8, 48, 71
Democratic elitism 62–63
Department of Education and Science
  (DES) 8, 10, 14, 71
Despot 28, 71
Dissidents 63, 71

Education 7, 10, 35, 39, 40, 42, 62
Education Act (1944) 12
Elected representative 10, 62, 71
Elections 67
Electorate 10, 46
Elites 62, 63
Elite theory 62, 71
Equal Pay Act (1970) 16, 30, 31, 57
Equal Opportunities Commission (EOC)
  22, 23, 71

Ethnicity 33, 71
Ethnic minority groups 12, 35
Exploitation 23, 56, 71
Executive 69
Extended family 24, 27, 31, 71

Factory Acts 56–57
Family 24–32
Feminism 30
Force 20, 50, 53
Free market 56, 71
Freedom 36, 57, 64, 66–67

Gender 3, 4, 15–23
General Practitioners (GPs) 55–56
Glasgow University Media Group 43
GLC 37
Government 1, 4, 5, 7, 8, 10, 12, 13, 22,
  23, 45, 46, 56, 61, 62, 64, 65, 66, 68

Hartman, P & Husband, C 35
Hereditary peers 69, 71
Hierarchy 58, 72
Housework 19, 30
House of Commons 68, 69, 72
House of Lords 54, 72

ILEA 40
Income differentials 52, 72
Independent schools 13–14
Industrial action 58, 72
Industrial disputes 52–53, 60, 72

Judiciary 69

Labour party 7, 11, 30, 42, 64
Language 21–22
Legislation 54, 57, 68, 72
Legislature 69
Liberal party 11
Liberal/Social Democratic Alliance 65
Liberal democracy 64
Life peers 69, 72
Local authorities 10, 13
Lucas Plan 59–60

Magazines 18, 24
Manipulate 20, 72
Mass media 19, 33, 34–35, 44–50
Members of Parliament (MPs) 2, 23, 35,
  56, 65, 68
Middle class 1, 12, 27
Military government 69, 72

Nationality Act (1981) 39
Neill, A S 25
Newspapers 21, 34, 35, 44–50, 54
Nuclear family 24, 28, 72

Official Secrets Act (1911) 68
Oligarchy 62

Parliament 2, 22, 23, 72
Participative direct democracy 25, 61, 72
Patriarchy 23, 26, 72

Patrials 39, 72
Party politics 7, 11, 72
Pay negotiations 52, 72
Peers 54, 72
Political activity 1, 2, 3, 22, 52
Politics of everyday life 1, 23
Political parties 10, 11, 23, 65–66
Power 2–5, 8, 10, 13, 14, 16–18, 21–25,
  31, 33, 35, 45–46, 50, 53, 54, 56, 62,
  68, 69, 72
Powerful 5, 21, 26
Powerless 5, 23, 53, 69
Powell, Enoch 34
Pressure groups 53, 54, 64–65, 72
Promotional groups 64
Protective groups 64–65
Proletarian 63, 72
Proportional representation 65

Race 3, 4, 33
Racism 33–40
Race Relations Acts (1965, 1968 & 1976)
  39
Representative democracy 10, 72
Revolution 63, 72

Sanctions 9
Schooling 7–14
Sex Discrimination Act (1975) 16, 22, 23,
  30, 57
Sexism 40, 72
Social class 1, 3, 4, 12
Social Democratic Party (SDP) 11
Socialization 16–18
Spender, Dale 22
State 44, 72
Status 4, 12, 13, 16, 21, 26, 51, 52, 53,
  54–56, 72
Stereotypes 15, 16, 17, 18, 34, 73
Stone, Lawrence 28
Symmetrical family 25
Status quo 43, 73

Television 24, 34, 35, 44–50
Totalitarian 63, 73
Trade unions 53, 57–58, 64
Trade Union Congress (TUC) 53, 73
Tripartite system 12–13, 73

Unemployment 30, 31, 35, 38, 59

Value 5, 12, 32, 33
Viewers and Listeners Association 50
Violence 20–21
Voters 10, 67–68

Willmott & Young 25
Withdraw labour 53, 73
Women's movement 23
Work 27, 51–60
Working class 1, 12, 13, 27, 31, 62